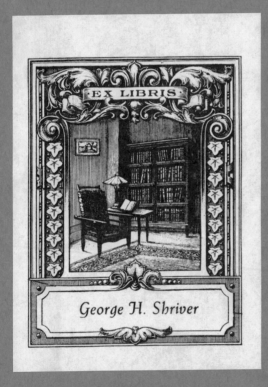

Religion and the American Nation

George H. Shriver
Lecture Series
in Religion
in American History
No. 1

RELIGION AND THE AMERICAN NATION

Historiography and History

John F. Wilson

The University of Georgia Press
Athens & London

© 2003 by the University of Georgia Press
Athens, Georgia 30602
All rights reserved
Designed by Louise OFarrell
Set in 10/16 Aldus
Printed and bound by Maple-Vail
The paper in this book meets the guidelines for
permanence and durability of the Committee on
Production Guidelines for Book Longevity of the
Council on Library Resources.

Printed in the United States of America

07   06   05   04   03   c   5   4   3   2   1

Library of Congress Cataloging-in-Publication Data
Wilson, John Frederick.
Religion and the American nation : historiography
and history / John F. Wilson.
p. cm. — (George H. Shriver lecture series in religion
in American history ; no. 1)
Includes bibliographical references and index.
ISBN 0-8203-2289-x (alk. paper)
1. United States—Religion. 2. United
States—Religion—Historiography. I. Title. II. Series.
BL2525.W54 2003
200'.973—dc21
2002152985

British Library Cataloging-in-Publication Data available

CONTENTS

FOREWORD

This volume contains the inaugural lectures of the George H. Shriver Lectures: Religion in American History, delivered at Stetson University on January 25–26, 2000. This lecture series has been endowed by Dr. George Shriver, professor emeritus of history at Georgia Southern University, in appreciation for his educational experience as an undergraduate at Stetson University. Sponsored by the Department of Religious Studies and the Department of History, this series joins together two of Dr. Shriver's academic passions: religious studies and history. Dr. Shriver is not just an observer of religious history; he is himself a scholarly analyst and chronicler of America's religious traditions. A professor for forty-one years, he is the author of numerous books and publications, including *Philip Schaff: Christian Scholar and Ecumenical Prophet*, *Contemporary Reflections on the Medieval Christian Tradition*, *From Science to Theology*, and *American Religious Heretics*. His most recent work, *Pilgrims through the Years: A Bicentennial History of First Baptist Church, Savannah, Georgia*, was recognized for its excellence by being awarded the Lilla Mills Hawes Award from the Georgia Historical Society in 2000 for the best book on local history (a cowinner). A member of Phi

Beta Kappa, Dr. Shriver has been the recipient of several honors and awards throughout his career, including being elected Professor of the Year, receiving the Award for Excellence in Research, being awarded the Ruffin Cup (Distinguished Award for Excellence in the Liberal Arts) from Georgia Southern University, and receiving the Distinguished Alumni Award from Stetson University.

The purpose of the Shriver Lectures is to bring to Stetson's campus distinguished scholars who will lecture on the role of religion in shaping America's past and present. Sydney Ahlstrom, in the preface to the Image Book edition of his work *A Religious History of the American People*, described the importance of understanding history, particularly, America's religious history. He wrote, "A nation that is unaware of its past bears an alarming similarity to a person suffering from amnesia: a crucial element of its being is lacking. . . . The present, after all, is but a thin film on the past, an imaginary figment; while the future exists only as a possibility—or a negation. In a certain sense, therefore, we all live and have our being in the past" (15). Through the generosity of George Shriver in endowing this lecture series, perhaps less of that "crucial element"—the past—will be deficient from our understanding.

Stetson University was honored to have Dr. John Wilson deliver the inaugural Shriver Lectures. Dean of the Graduate School, and Agate Brown and George L. Collord Professor of Religion at Princeton University, Dr. Wilson has spent his career as a scholarly observer of America's religious heritage.

The recipient of many academic honors, he is a member of Phi Beta Kappa and a recipient of a Fulbright Grant and of a Guggenheim Fellowship, and he was a Fellow of the National Humanities Center. His numerous scholarly writings have explored the influence of religion in American culture from the Puritans to civil religion. He is the author or editor of several works, including *Public Religion in American Culture, Pulpit in Parliament: Puritanism during the English Civil Wars, 1640–1648,* and *Church and State in America: A Bibliographical Guide.*

In this three-part lecture series entitled Religion and the American Nation: Historiography and History, Dr. Wilson lays a solid foundation upon which future Shriver Lectures can be built. His lectures explore the various ways that historians of religion have examined and analyzed America's religious landscape. Arguing that the true beginnings of the historiography of religion in America are found in the nineteenth century, Wilson, in his first lecture, highlights the contributions of writers such as Philip Schaff, Peter Mode, William Warren Sweet, Sidney Mead, Clifton Olmstead, Winthrop Hudson, and Sydney Ahlstrom, tracing the origins and development of self-conscious historiography about religion in the United States. Throughout this initial period, the controlling narrative for understanding American religious history was the Protestant story, specifically, Puritanism. The second lecture begins chronologically where the first ended, tracing the historiographical study of religion in America after the time of Sydney Ahlstrom. Wilson describes how new narrative versions of America's religious history began to appear, narrative approaches that stressed the pluralistic character of America's religious history. This religious pluralism was not a new phenomenon in American religion but was present from the very beginning, although often overshadowed or completely ignored by the dominant Protestant narrative. In addition, new paradigms and methodologies from the social sciences shaped how historians analyzed and told America's religious history. In the third and final lecture, Wilson explores the question of whether there is a particular "American religion," that is, whether the American nation has itself become a religious object. Here he deals not only with the more conventional idea of civil religion but also with the various ways in which contemporary American society functions as a religion.

A special word of thanks is due to George Shriver, both for his generous endowment of the lectures and for his attendance at the lectures along with his wife, Cathy. Their charm and graciousness added to the pleasure of the event. Appreciation is also expressed to the following: Dr. H. Douglas Lee, president of Stetson University, for his support of and interest in the Shriver Lectures; Professor Kevin O'Keefe of the Department of History and Professor Paul Jerome Croce of the Department of American Studies for their assistance in planning and coordinating the lectures; Lisa Guenther, Mary Anne Rogers, and Colleen Cooper for handling many of the details to ensure that the lectures and Dr. Wilson's visit went smoothly; the many students, faculty, staff, and people of the community who attended the lectures and shared in this intellectual enrichment; and Nicole Mitchell and Sarah McKee of the University of Georgia Press for assistance in the publication of these lectures.

> *Mitchell G. Reddish*
> *Chair, George H. Shriver Lectures Committee*
> *Stetson University*

ACKNOWLEDGMENTS

I wish to thank Stetson University, especially its Department of Religious Studies under the leadership of Mitchell Reddish and its Department of History, for the invitation to deliver the Shriver Lectures in January 2000. I considered it a great honor to inaugurate the series and very much appreciated the opportunity to explore the issues that are addressed in the following pages. The published chapters follow directly from the three individual lectures, each one of which developed a particular theme. I was especially gratified by George Shriver's presence at each of the lectures because he generously provided for this series. He has been an associate and friend for many years, and the invitation to give this series of lectures at Stetson University held special meaning for me.

Religion and the American Nation

INTRODUCTION

The Historiography of Religion in America

Gᴇᴏʀɢᴇ Sʜʀɪᴠᴇʀ has given the title Religion in American History to this series of lectures. This gives each lecturer wonderfully elastic scope, permitting, if not inviting, attention to a range of subjects. Across a span of years, I can imagine that successive lecturers may choose to focus their presentations more narrowly as well as more broadly. In any case, unconstrained by what others might have done, I had the opportunity as the inaugural lecturer to chart the first course of Shriver Lectures. In this spirit, I proposed to review an interlocking set of issues rather than address a narrower topic concerning religion in American history.

It will not escape the reader's notice that both the book's title and the subtitle are compound—*Religion and the American Nation* and *Historiography and History*—and that is deliberate. In effect, one member of each pair delineates the subject matter, while the other member serves as a regulating or controlling reference. Let me elaborate briefly. Religion, or even religion in American history, is a broad rubric that allows for a range of approaches, for example, to literature, to art, to music, or to the economy. By relating religion to the term *the American nation*, I intend to focus on religion in relationship to the political organization of the society rather than primarily to its cultural or aesthetic dimensions or to economic ones—other possible regulating categories that might shape the inquiry. While that is an old-fashioned starting point, in accord with earlier generations of general historiography, I hope to demonstrate that it need not unduly constrain our imaginations or limit our explorations. It should be clear, however, that I am not primarily concerned with nationalism or with the American nation. Were either of those subjects the primary topic, it would have the effect of making attention to religion only secondary or possibly even incidental.

This subject of religion and the American nation invites a special observation. Some of those who advocate understanding America in terms of its "exceptionalism" commonly argue that the American nation is unique or sui generis precisely because it is a nation defined by means of reference to an idea or ideal.[1] This claim contrasts sharply with the assumption that the identities of virtually all other nations have been rooted in language, land, or lordly activity, the typical reference points in tracing origins of peoples and states. That the American nation has a unique status is not a proposition I wish either to lift up for extended review or to defend in detail. But it does suggest that there are grounds in the very terms that define American nationhood that make the place of religion within it unusual, to say the least, perhaps even unique among the nations of the world.[2] Using the American nation as a regulating limit also makes it evident that this discussion will not relate to our neighbors to the south or north—as relevant as the general topic of religion and the new worlds of the Americas would prove to be, especially if explored comparatively. Indeed, that topic would be a fit and wonderful subject for future Shriver Lectures.

In a parallel way, the subtitle links historiography with history. My primary interest is in the historiography of religion in America, that is, how the topic has been written about. But the regulating reference in this case is history, that is, the flow of events that comprise the stuff attended to in historiography. So although the compound title and subtitle have significant roles to play in the construction of these lectures, the basic subject matter of this series will be the historiography of religion in the United States.

Following the original three-lecture format, I also utilize three chapters to frame coherent segments of a progressive discussion. The first chapter considers religion in America in terms of the long tradition of writing about religion that began in the early decades of American political independence. This account brings the story down through several centuries until roughly the 1970s. Given the scale and complexity of the subject, this account of the historiography of religion in America is necessarily selective, even arbitrarily so, rather than comprehensive. A number of major contributors, active participants in the story, have simply been passed over or left out of it altogether. My overriding objective has been to frame the larger picture rather than do justice to the details, a task that would be wholly impossible in the limited format of this series.[3]

The subtitle for the initial chapter, "The Long Shadow of the Puritans," signals that, however many twists and turns we locate and discuss, it is useful to recognize a topic that provides the underlying continuity of this historiography. This basic theme, common to one and a half centuries of history writing, tracks our comprehension of religion in American history back into one or another interpretation of the Puritan influence. Accordingly, one question lurking beneath the surface of these chapters concerns how we understand Puritanism under a double burden. On the one hand, Puritanism and related terms have been widely utilized (indeed, repeatedly overutilized) historically to define at least *a* if not *the* terminus a quo of accounts of religion in American history, while on the other, it has been repudiated in popular culture for its presumed substance and, among current students of American religion and culture, for its hegemonic implications. One objective of this volume is to suggest that the term and the reference may be rehabilitated so that they are useful in the ongoing historiographical effort devoted to American religion.

In the second chapter, titled "Religions in America," I turn to some more recent responses to or reactions against this tradition of historiography. In the last decades, not a few scholars have sought to construct accounts of religion by attempting explicitly to ground them in ways that seek either to avoid or to trump references to Puritanism. The subtitle of this chapter suggests two common strategies in these multiple efforts. One strategy has been to develop these accounts by proposing that a cluster of multiple narratives serves the purpose of historiography better than a forced interpretation of American religion as one encompassing story basically deriving from Puritanism. The other strategy or approach has been to adapt paradigms from the social sciences to identify mechanisms or basic patterns of action and reaction that undergird different religious episodes in American history. Of course, a fundamental question may be asked about both of these moves; namely, do these shifts or new starting points in fact transcend reference(s) to the Puritans and/or Puritanism as a means of providing the basic template for religion in American history?

In the third chapter, titled "Religion(s) of America," I explore what might be termed the religiously generative dimension of the American society, assuming that this nation (like other social orders) embodies such a potential. On this point it can be argued that, comparable to other human collectivities, American society entails "attachment mechanisms" that are usefully delineated as "religious." The somewhat flip subtitle, "From Civil Religion to Milling at the Mall," is intended to suggest the extreme range of behaviors, if not of beliefs, that may plausibly be understood as religious aspects of residence in American society and as signals of participation in its polity. Accordingly, there are many subjects to visit and explore in this compressed endeavor, and there is no more appropriate starting point than turning our attention to the long shadow of the Puritans.

RELIGION IN AMERICA

The Long Shadow of the Puritans

SERIOUS HISTORY WRITING about religion and the role it played in the new American nation began in the nineteenth century. Indeed, it was among foreign visitors or occasionally among Americans who were exposed to other societies and cultures that an impulse took root to note and begin to puzzle over the place and significance of religion in society as it took shape in the New World. Alexis de Tocqueville stands as representative among names of the first kind. His *Democracy in America* has come to be a universal sourcebook for those wishing to prove almost anything about the new United States.[1] With respect to religion, however, there is a prima facie case that, in the course of his travels, Tocqueville discovered a degree of religious engagement among Americans that struck him as truly noteworthy and critically important for an understanding of the new society. In volume 1, his occasional references to American religion build to wonderment—if not bewilderment—at this discovery. In volume 2, he steps back and systematically reflects on his encounters with religion.[2] However celebrated his insights, it is certainly not clear that he got the relationship of religion and the political society entirely right. John Noonan has playfully argued this case through imagining a sister, "Angelique," whose alternate account trumps her brother's insights on this subject.[3] Indeed, some decades ago, Perry Miller opined that Tocqueville's views were overvalued and that a somewhat later visitor (whom we shall discuss momentarily) much more effectively and accurately delineated the subject.[4] But the question of importance for us ought to be, Why did religion become identified as a significant ingredient in the American society and nation and sufficiently recognized as such to require treatment as a separate subject only in the nineteenth century?

Surely, there had been historical accounts of religion in the preceding centuries. Indeed, some might argue that early colonial settlers' self-understandings were predominantly informed by theologically directed views of religion's significance. That seems to be a fair judgment. Pre-nineteenth-century interpretations of America's role in world history typically derived from schemes of meaning that privileged biblical revelation. In such accounts, the discovery of the New World and its exploitation were linked to Providence-directed destinies.[5] Formally considered, while accounts like these could be the basis for frameworks of historical meaning, nonetheless, they do not necessarily qualify as exhibits of critical history writing or antecedents of modern historiography.

In *A Loss of Mastery: Puritan Historians in Colonial America*, published in 1966, one of his many books that stands apart from the bulk of his writings by virtue of its concern with colonial American materials, Peter Gay delineated with great sensitivity the peculiarities of the writing of history in the prenational period.[6] Not surprisingly, he traced a progressive decline from the historically grounded accounts of the earliest of New England settlers, especially that of William Bradford, through the more formal chronicles of Cotton Mather, to the theological framework Jonathan Edwards set out in his sermon series, A History of the Work of Redemption. Gay argues, in effect, that the initial parochial-level discussions like Bradford's conveyed authentic historical insights in discussing the subject matter of the early settlements and thus connected with modern historiographical concerns. But at the same time, this quality of realism was progressively, and irretrievably, lost as increasingly grand theological systems of meaning came to the fore and took up the burden of framing historical events.[7]

Gay's judgment seems altogether right, and a close reading of the relevant texts helps to make that amply clear. In the immediate context of the current study, however, the significant point is not that the materials of religion were overlooked in colonial America. Instead, their interpretation was raised to an increasingly theological plane rather than treated historically and thus more closely in accord with what would come to be the canons of critical historiography. One of the more interesting persons attending to the relevant materials was Hannah Adams, a schoolteacher and an early and formidable compiler who published an *Alphabetical Compendium* as well as dictionaries of religious sects and groups.[8] In this case, the subject matter of religion was certainly foremost but necessarily set in another kind of universal framework. Adams was not exploring these materials as exhibits that were peculiarly tied to the American nation. Thus it seems necessary and appropriate that we should look to the nineteenth century to chart the true beginnings of the historiography of religion in America, that is, self-conscious interpretation in historical terms of the religious behaviors and beliefs peculiar to the nation that formed as the political construct we conventionally label "America."[9]

At the outset of this chapter, I noted that the most acute nineteenth-century insights into the place of religion in American history could be attributed to individuals of two sorts. One kind came to the United States as visitors or as immigrants. In short, like Tocqueville, they experienced the national life of America as aliens. The other and even smaller group comprised Americans who had sufficient experience of other societies and nations to develop at least an implicitly critical perspective of their own. If Tocqueville represents the first type, a rough contemporary, Robert Baird, stands for the other. Baird was a Presbyterian who served on an extended missionary assignment in Europe in the early decades of the nineteenth century. While living overseas and undertaking to explain his own nation to Europeans, he wrote what deserves to be highlighted as among the very first studies of religion in American history.[10] Breaking with the framework of the earlier tradition of writing that was heavily determined by theological commitments, Baird produced something of a chronological account of religious movements and bodies (in contrast to Adams's inventories). He also turned his attention to Italy as well as to northern European countries and the West Indies in writing accounts that were in some respects comparable.[11] Baird seems to have been urged to share his study of his homeland's religious life with his fellow Americans.

We have already noted that Perry Miller advanced as his opinion that another foreign-born author, a Swiss scholar named Philip Schaff, actually had come to understand religion in America far more acutely than had Alexis de Tocqueville in his work.[12] Schaff was a somewhat reluctant immigrant to the New World. He would have preferred to advance along a career path within established European universities and churches rather than relocating to the Pennsylvania frontier. But he accepted a call to Mercersburg, Pennsylvania, having been recruited to the faculty of a new seminary, in effect, to serve as an ornament for the German Reformed Church. Reacting to the regnant revivalism of the time and in concert with his colleague John Williamson Nevin, who was himself a well-known and trenchant critic of this American religious invention, Schaff developed one of the more noteworthy theological "schools of thought" or parties in American history.[13] The Mercersburg Theology articulated a romantic alternative to the reductively instrumental program of revivalism. (I use the term *romantic* to describe a cultural moment rather than to designate a fictional strategy.)[14] In particular, this school of thought valued symbol and myth as critical ingredients of vital tradition, especially necessary to sustain religious sensibility and perhaps particularly so on the American frontier.[15] I trace here only one small element of Schaff's scholarly production, namely, his comments about the strange system of providing for religion that he discovered—and came to appreciate and wholeheartedly endorse—in the New World.

While reluctantly coming to accept that he would be tied to the North American side of the Atlantic, Philip Schaff nonetheless remained connected to Europe throughout much of his career. He frequently visited Germany and went on to make extensive use of the Vatican Archives in his later career as the leading church historian in the United States after the Civil War.[16] The essays that hold the most interest for us are published versions of lectures about America that he wrote for and delivered to German audiences.[17] Perry Miller, who republished these occasional pieces in the middle of the twentieth century, claimed that Schaff had deeper insight into the transformation that religion had undergone in the New World than others had achieved (e.g., Tocqueville, who could have benefited from his "sister's" corrective tutoring on the subject).

In what lay the superiority of Schaff's insight as far as Miller was concerned? Primarily, it was his understanding that freeing religion from dependence upon and obligation to the state had an immensely salutary effect.[18] Voluntary religion was, so to speak, something new under the sun, at least as it had shined on European lands. Rather than failing to attract members or falling into irrelevance, religion that was reconceived along voluntary lines had proved to be immensely energizing. Schaff emphasized the contrast he observed between the relative absence of churches in the great cities of the Old World and their presence and prominence in the cities of the New World. This perception led him toward the end of his career to draft a significant essay in which he undertook to analyze church and state in the United States as a major innovation in Western history.[19]

Schaff himself was very much committed to a Christian, indeed, broadly evangelical, view of human history. He believed that Christianity had played a significantly progressive role in Western civilization and that it was part of—at least partial explanation for—the progress achieved by the West. While living through the Civil War (and in the process experiencing the closing of his host institution), Schaff relocated to New York City. Eventually, he served as a much honored professor at the Union Theological Seminary in that city at the culmination of his career.

As already suggested, a progressive view of history was embedded in his consciousness as well as in his history writing.[20] This triumphalism was to be challenged and finally overturned in the twentieth century. In this connection it is important to note that liberal canons of history writing had to be modified as a necessary prerequisite for the eventual development of a tradition of critical history writing about American religion. However explicitly secular progressive views of history might have been, they also embodied—almost as a shadowed formulation—the forward-facing impulse so central to theologically informed historical schemes in which the millennium played a prominent part.

Schaff served as one of the general editors for an ambitious thirteen-volume project sponsored by the American Society of Church History. This series of studies, published between 1893 and 1897, recounted the history of each major family of denominations in the United States as the turn of the twentieth century approached. Henry K. Carroll drew on the 1890 census when he wrote the first volume, *The Religious Forces of the United States,* while the concluding thirteenth volume was written by Leonard Woolsey Bacon.[21] Entitled *A History of American Christianity,* it suggested a very broad view of the subject within the culture as a whole.[22] Indeed, Bacon's account went so far as to recognize the role of pre-Columbian elements in American religious history. This was a fresh be-

ginning point for an encompassing narrative and a markedly
new perspective within religious historiography.

Finally, it is possible to locate and identify in the twentieth
century a strong historiographic tradition of systematic study
concerning religion in the history of the United States. The
University of Chicago was the preeminent institutional home
for this undertaking, at least in its early years.[23] Itself a new
university, dedicated in its Divinity School to represent Protestantism as central to the modern world, it aspired to be
among the world's great centers of learning. A commitment to
the historical study of religion took root there and in a very
special modality: religion, historically considered, was taken
to be thoroughly embedded in society. Through the leadership
of Shirley Jackson Case, the Divinity School fostered powerful
and deep-ranging scholarship about the early centuries of the
Christian tradition. It was only natural that the same assumptions and historiographical conventions that were worked out
at Chicago for the study of early Christianity should be considered appropriate to interpreting religion in American society. Peter G. Mode was the first practitioner of this new
method, and in his hands its beginnings were exceptionally
promising.[24]

Mode is one of the more interesting figures in the chain of
those studying religion in American history. Teaching at Chicago and working in a historiographical era deeply influenced
by Frederick Jackson Turner's "frontier thesis," Mode published, in 1921, a remarkable sourcebook that brought together

a broad array of bibliographical evidence related to American church history.[25] He also composed a small monograph constructed upon these resources.[26] He then vanished from sight. Oral tradition has it that dimensions of his personal life were not in accord with the expectations governing faculty appointments to the University of Chicago's Divinity School. He apparently disappeared into a career selling insurance. A great loss this turned out to be, for Mode's sourcebook and monograph are evidence that in his mature work he would have exploited the frontier paradigm in a sophisticated way and to great advantage. In some respects, a less-well-known figure, Henry K. Rowe, whose teaching career was at Andover-Newton Seminary, came as close as any to continuing this impulse, although his writing was only a pale reflection of the promise Mode's work had held out.[27]

At the University of Chicago, the challenge was picked up by William Warren Sweet, who for decades published widely on the topic of religion both in colonial and national America.[28] Sweet also took the frontier as defining the essence of the challenge to religion posed in the United States. He and his students tracked through vast amounts of material bearing on major traditions as they encountered and were transformed by the conditions of frontier life, compiling or assembling straightforward accounts along denominational lines. At one level, Sweet surely was working in continuity with Mode's program, but his publications had a predictable quality, failing to make contact with the state-of-the-art historiog-raphy of the time.

Another figure with ties to the University of Chicago came closer to making good on the promise latent in Mode's work, although not through emphasizing the frontier as the central interpretive principle. If Mode compiled a substantial guide to available data and literature, laying the foundation for a com-prehensive analysis of religion in America, Sidney Mead, who died in 1999, stands as another kind of history writer.[29] As a historiographer, Mead was the quintessential essayist, an au-thor who, through carefully posed questions and well-crafted arguments, moved the writing of history forward by reformu-lating intellectual frameworks and recasting the search for data. His most widely used volume was a compilation of es-says published in 1963 as *The Lively Experiment;* the title in-dicates Mead's consuming interest in the nature of American society as it related to religion. For Mead, the "experiment" incorporated dimensions associated with the hyperindividual-istic religious enthusiasm of Roger Williams as well as those assumptions rooted in the Enlightenment that had been voiced most compellingly by Thomas Jefferson, archchampion of religious freedom.[30] The American Republic had been founded on principles that derived from both evangelicalism and the Enlightenment. In Mead's view, America's uniqueness lay in its commitment to an idea or ideal, and as such it was the "last, best hope of the earth." Mead's essays are still profitably read for the rigor with which they parse the nation's inner or spiritual life.

I have reviewed and commented on the historiography of American religion, and beyond Mead my story moves quickly into an era marked by a series of overviews or compendia published by numerous authors. Baird had aspired to undertake such a project, but it was not a task that even a prolific writer and researcher such as Philip Schaff could accept. Had he done so, Schaff would surely have played out the theme of America as the locus for the reunion of Catholic and Protestant Christianities. He thought of this as an eventuality in which the particularities of each would together make a whole greater than the sum of the parts.[31] Had Peter Mode continued to work in the vein he had opened up, he might well have produced the first modern study of religion in American history, organizing it in terms of a theoretical problematic: the challenge of the frontier and the response, the adaptation, and the remaking of religion (especially Christianity) in America. Although in broad terms Sweet embraced this as his mission, his work did not incorporate the interplay of theory or models and data and thus failed to connect with the broader developments in general history writing. As a consequence, his many and extensive publications were rather wooden in their organization. Mead by design did not propose to write such a compendium. By the middle of the twentieth century, however, the field of religion in American history was ripe for such efforts, and a series of writings of this sort can be identified in the decades immediately following World War II.

Honor of place might be given somewhat arbitrarily to Clifton Olmstead, long-time professor at George Washington University. In a volume that was transparently imagined (and undoubtedly developed) as a course textbook, Olmstead undertook to tell the story of religion in America as a narrative account, moving from religion during the American nation's beginnings to contemporary times.[32] It exemplified very clearly the move to seek a unified field in the study of religion in American history through the means of narrative-based accounts. While something of the same impulse was evident in Sweet's books, it was not deemed a necessary device by Baird—or, for that matter, by Tocqueville or Schaff. We might opine that the notion of a controlling narrative breaks the surface with Olmstead's book, and it remains the approach around which—or in reaction to which—the remainder of this and succeeding accounts of religion in American history were written through the subsequent years of the twentieth century.

Just as the discussion thus far has been schematic, proceeding by means of selective reference rather than exhaustive detail, the rest of this chapter necessarily picks and chooses among possible subjects. Olmstead's book was accompanied by others that effectively framed American religious history in the same extended-narrative format. One of the most widely used of this genre is that by Winthrop Hudson. His *Religion in America* was first published in 1965, and it has gone through six editions and uncounted printings.[33] Based on the same overall frame used by Olmstead or, for that matter, Sweet, it traces the "story of religion" from the earliest coherent colonial settlements in New England to the multiple religious preferences exhibited in the United States at mid–twentieth century. Elements in the story include the origins of and the variations among the Protestant groupings, the rise of the Roman Catholic Church through immigration and the triumph of the Irish religious leadership in that community, the complex and basically triadic structure of the Jewish community, the diversification of Protestant bodies, and the frustrations encountered in attempts to foster ecumenical initiatives or interfaith activities. To review the successive editions of Hudson's book is to watch the progressive broadening of awareness about how religious life became more complex in the postwar era as reflected through periodically revisiting the historical materials. Like Olmstead's volume, Hudson's was designed as a textbook to serve as the spine in the organization of a course. Each of the chapters is of roughly equivalent length, and the total number reflects the typical number of class meetings in a conventional term or semester.

Alongside a fully developed text like Hudson's, we can also find related publications that aspire to capsule and present the materials of religion in American history through selected readings or casebooks. One of the most attractive examples is

Conrad Cherry's *God's New Israel: Religious Interpretations of American Destiny*. Initially published in 1971, it has been revised and reissued as recently as 1998.[34] This particular collection works well in concert with the textbooks mentioned above and other similar products. An even more ambitious teaching book is a two-volume compilation of source materials selected and introduced by three highly regarded authors: H. Shelton Smith, Robert T. Handy, and Lefferts Loetscher.[35] While explicitly titled *American Christianity*, thus seeming to have a restrictive focus that might be thought to exclude wide ranges of data (especially those not Christian), in fact, the volumes' scope is reasonably inclusive. They might have been better served by another title that would have emphasized their incorporation of religious subjects beyond those nominally Christian.

Truncated specimens—monographs that deal with a central or core subject matter within the overall narrative and that are treated in such a way as to confirm and undergird that framework—also represent this same period of historical interpretation. For example, Martin E. Marty's *Righteous Empire* was crafted to tell the story of the dominant Protestant impulse that was at once dynamic and powerful and yet changing in the course of the nineteenth century. But this story presupposed—and in doing that reinforced—the larger narrative laid out in the fuller accounts.[36] Robert T. Handy's *A Christian America*, published almost concurrently, might be identified as a parallel narrative line that diverged in particulars from

Marty's account but that in its own way supported the more inclusive basic story line set out in the textbooks.[37] There is even a sense that a study that breaks decisively with this literature while at the same time drawing from it and in the end reinforcing it belongs to this genre; this is the fascinating sociological essay by Will Herberg, *Protestant-Catholic-Jew*.[38] The ordering of the faith communities in the title suggests the book's internal connection to those narrative accounts of religion in American history that came to maturity in the post–World War II era. I return to Herberg's study in the third chapter, but I introduce it here to emphasize the larger point made in these paragraphs before moving on. That point is that the comprehensive historical account of religion in America was expressed not only in and through the efforts of many authors to encompass the whole in a single narrative but also in countless articles published in journals and secondary monographs on limited topics as well as through ancillary literature like sourcebooks and readers.[39]

This entire impulse was nowhere more impressively summarized than in an inclusive and magisterial work by a prominent historian of the era. Sydney Ahlstrom completed his doctoral work on the Unitarians at Harvard, but his career was largely played out at Yale, where he taught for several decades. He held concurrent academic appointments at Yale in three arts and sciences departments (American studies, history, and religious studies) as well as serving on the faculty of its Divinity School. Ahlstrom had extensive indirect influence on the study of religion in American history through his many graduate students, whose writing and research shaped an era of scholarship and teaching, as well as very direct impact through his writings. Chief among them was a volume that stood both as the culmination of this historiographical impulse we have been describing—the challenge of achieving an inclusive critical narrative history of religion in America—and at the same time as the demonstration that such a paradigm was basically problematic.

A Religious History of the American People, published in 1972, was, and remains, a remarkable volume.[40] Comprising 63 separate chapters and totaling 1,160 pages, it was driven by a commitment to enlarge received views by giving attention to the marginal and overlooked. Framed in terms of cultural as well as political and social history, the book defies easy description. A consummate teller of stories, Ahlstrom drew his reader into a fascinating world that compelled attention. At one level, he recounted concurrent narratives about relatively isolated and distinct events in the religious history of the people who constitute America. At another level, each of these stories had its place within a master narrative. Ahlstrom himself identified the subject of this macroaccount as the great four hundred–year period of dominant Protestant influence beginning with the accession of Elizabeth I to the throne of England in 1560. Researching and writing the volume in the 1950s and 1960s, he proposed that this great period might have ended, so to speak, with the election of John F. Kennedy to the American presidency, the first Roman Catholic to hold that office. Ahlstrom believed that the reach of his macronarrative was essentially exhausted, implying that the theme would no longer serve to bring order and meaning to any continuation of his story. Useful as a retrospective organizing principle, it might cease to be a vital organizing principle in comprehending religion in successive decades of the nation's history.

Two interesting discussions open out from this point. One concerns interpretive principles, in this case, whether any macronarrative continues to be viable after its social base has been eliminated. If, to adopt this perspective, the Protestant hegemony was no longer as deeply at work in the society after 1960, would not any great account of the American people's religious life necessarily be written in terms of a new point of view that would presumably be more encompassing?[41] The theme of secularization, for example, might replace that of a Protestant hegemony. The other discussion concerns the data; could it have been that the great Catholic tradition descending from ancient Rome was in fact becoming "Protestantized"? Suppose a nominal Catholic who was president in fact behaved and acted more like a Protestant? What if, within several years of the election in question (1960), a "stealth pope" was installed in Saint Peter's See who would undertake a thorough renovation of Catholic tradition? Would the great "quadricentennium," as Ahlstrom was known to term it, in fact have come to an end? He left such questions unaddressed and unanswered in his magisterial book. My point in centering the culmination of this chapter upon it is that *A Religious History of the American People* at once exemplifies an era in which narrative accounts of religion in American history were produced and refined while also serving to bring it to a close. Soon after Ahlstrom's opus was published, searching, indeed vexing, questions about coherence and continuity swept through discussions among the scholars working with this subject. That development will comprise the central thread of the second chapter, but in closing we should reflect on the subtitle of this chapter that has served as a subtext throughout it: "The Long Shadow of the Puritans."

Why are the Puritans, and why is Puritanism, elevated to a place of privilege in this discussion? As is true of so many seemingly simple questions, an adequate reply requires that attention be given to several levels of response. At the most elemental level, the Puritans loomed large because the movement served as a point of departure for rendering coherent conventional accounts of the transit of European and largely British civilization, especially its religious components, to the New World.[42] But what happens when it is recognized that the transit of civilizations involved the entire Atlantic basin, with peoples from Africa and Europe interacting upon both the South and North American continents with indigenous populations?[43] This displacement of Puritans and Puritanism has necessarily reflected a much enlarged critical perspective on the ingredients that went into creating the great range of societies in the New World as well as in the American nation.

At a secondary level, references to the Puritans reflected the hegemonic role of British-Protestant culture in the early years of the evolving United States. But what happens when it is recognized that the content of American culture is continuously evolving, in fact, explicitly reflecting, often in partial and distorted ways, not only the numerous European and African peoples who have made America their own but newer Asian and Middle Eastern immigrants as well?[44]

Finally, however, there is the possibility for making critical use of the reference. The Puritans as folk and Puritanism as an intensive movement, rendered intelligible through understanding their religious self-descriptions, may display prototypical dynamics for how religion has functioned in American history.[45] Taken in this third sense, reference to Puritanism may turn out to be useful long after its direct—or even mediated—influence has effectively ceased. This question, then, concerning the uses that critical historiography makes of selected cases and instances so that they serve as paradigms, will necessarily hover in the background of the succeeding chapters in this study.

RELIGIONS
IN AMERICA

Narratives and Paradigms

C HAPTER 1 sketched the origins and development of self-
conscious historiography about religion in the United States.
The roots of this intellectual project trace back in precritical
history writing to theologically framed discussions of divine
intentions for society in the New World, but only in the nineteenth century did the historiography of religion emerge as a
subject for formal study. We picked up the story as the impulse was transformed into what at first may have been incidental attention to religion and its role in American society.
Subsequently, the interest became a continuing effort to interpret American religious history. Beginning with a passing reference to William Bradford, the chapter closed with reflections
on Sydney Ahlstrom, whose monumental *A Religious His-*

tory of the American People at once represented the maturation of this tradition and fully exemplified a comprehensive narrative account of the subject. At the same time, his work provided grounds for calling into question the ideal of rendering American religious history by means of a single narrative.

The burden of this chapter is to explore the historiographical study of religion in American history since Ahlstrom. This means tracing out several trajectories in terms of which scholarship has advanced the study of religion in American history in the last decades, roughly since 1970.[1] The chapter title indicates both an overall observation and an argument, namely that *religions* in American history—that is to say, the multiplicity of religious phenomena rather than their commonality as a phenomenon—have effectively become the subject. But the subtitle suggests that this quest has taken divergent paths or been carried by scholarly impulses deriving from different sources, so discussion of the interplay between multiple narratives and divergent paradigms provides the double axes for this chapter.

Before launching forth to explore these themes, it is important to supplement the discussion of the last chapter with reference to another dimension of the subject. I proposed that Ahlstrom represented the culmination of an era because the focus had been on an overall narrative account of religion in American history. From this perspective, his work was followed by a dramatic reconfiguration of the impulse to study religion in American history. Alternatively, I might have turned the subject in another direction by emphasizing a complementary side of the story, namely, the quite extraordinary expansion of interest in religious topics among historians generally. This signal development was, in fact, noted and framed in a well-known article that would serve as a symbolic marker that a new period was beginning even as the Ahlstrom volume is a marker that one was ending.

Henry May's article, published in the *American Historical Review* in 1964, was titled "The Recovery of American Religious History."[2] In it he charted the dramatic increase of studies in many genres—articles, monographs, books—concerned with religious subjects, phenomena, and related topics in American history. For him, this extensive literature represented a genuinely new phase in professional history writing about the United States, for it moved back into the center of scholarly discussions a subject that had been rather thoroughly marginalized in the development of that historiography. Interestingly enough, publications sponsored by the early American Historical Association in the late nineteenth century or contemporaneous papers delivered at meetings of this august professional organization frequently featured attention to religious topics, among others (often institutional studies based on available archives and data).[3] But in the course of the early decades of the twentieth century, there was a tendency to relegate religious topics to the provinces of the specialized societies that were dedicated to religious subjects, groups like the reconstituted American Society of Church

History and the American Catholic Historical Association.[4] By the 1960s, however, May believed that widespread and deeply probing research and writing concerned with religion in American history had reentered general historical writing.

In May's view, interest in the subject had emerged among "secular" historians at the same time that the central narrative that was commonplace among specialized religious historians had begun to fray. That narrative concerned the significance of *religion* understood essentially as varieties of Protestantism, exemplified by (if not genetically derived from) Puritanism.[5] The new interest among general historians attended much more to particular episodes or events involving *religions* understood more pluralistically. This chapter will not devote time or attention to argue in detail that what may *appear* to be a tension, if not a contradiction or even a paradox, in fact represented two sides of the same development: microstudies flourished, while macroaccounts languished. What really matters is that with respect to the historiography of religion in America, a new period began in the 1960s. That is the subject matter with which this chapter is concerned, and the remainder of it will be devoted to exploring that development.

One useful exhibit of this new period is a textbook that was written by a "new-style" historian of religion in America. Catherine Albanese received a Roman Catholic education, indeed, apparently considered a religious vocation as a teaching sister, before enrolling in the Divinity School at the University of Chicago to complete a doctoral program in American religious history. In addition to her extra-Protestant background, she became deeply influenced by history of religions perspectives that were then regnant at the Divinity School of the University of Chicago. This led to her first book, *Sons of the Fathers*, published in 1976, which concerned civil religion in the Revolutionary era—this was, of course, the year of the bicentennial celebration.[6] *Corresponding Motion*, a study of the Transcendentalists that represented her Chicago dissertation, quickly followed it.[7] But for the purposes of this chapter, Albanese's overview of religion(s) in American history, *America: Religions and Religion*, published in 1981, is the significant marker.[8]

The title suggests the two dimensions in which Albanese worked to parse the subject that concerns us. The plural form, "religions," coming first as it did in the subtitle, indicates how seriously she weighed the deep pluralism of these phenomena. Her account gives significant attention to Native Americans, for example, as well as to the reality of Spanish settlements, and she posits the latter's continuing influence in (and surely well beyond) the twentieth century, especially in the southwestern and western regions of the United States. She also explores the deep and continuing struggle between French and British imperialisms as well as the fundamental presence of and contributions by Americans of African descent, whatever their legal status. These features give this account a texture altogether different from those of Hudson, Ahlstrom, and others written in the older mold.[9] Proposing that America in its religious dimension was fundamentally plural puts a different frame around a range of historic and contemporary phenomena. It implies, for example, that indigenous movements should be accorded more independence than they are often credited with, be they Oneida Perfectionists, Utah Mormons, or followers of the Reverend Sun Myung Moon. Whether or not Albanese's intellectual interests actually ranged more broadly than Ahlstrom's, the net effect of her more open interpretive framework was to promote study of the great range and diversity of religious ideas and activities exhibited in American history in their own right.[10]

At the same time, Albanese's title signaled an interest in "religion," suggesting that no less significant to her, as someone who had drunk deeply at the history of religions well, were those phenomena that might derive from the dynamics of America as itself a community.[11] This other side of her interests is not surprising in light of her first book, which explicitly concerned the civil-religious dimensions of the Revolutionary era. This perspective also recognized that such impulses might be expressed through unitive Protestant impulses or by means of other quasi-religious movements. Indeed, Albanese imagined an American history in which dialectical relationships between religions and religion had ramified between as well as among disparate constitutive groups at different times and places. At Albanese's hands, the entire religious matrix of American society and culture manifested a three-dimensional quality that marked a major departure from the narrative-dependent style of the earlier comprehensive accounts, which, to be sure, continued to have useful lives.

In certain respects, Albanese's book taken by itself embodies the two separate impulses that I explore in the remainder of this chapter. One is the approach to American religious history that undertook to make the case that multiple narratives should replace a master narrative; the other is the approach that took seriously studies of religion among social scientists that propose how useful generic mechanisms or common dynamics can be to interpret American (as well as extra-American) religious phenomena. Such paradigms and typical constructs as "revitalization movements" or "millenarian movements," to cite two frequently used examples, served as templates that accommodated numerous and varying examples of particular events or episodes in American history as well as many other instances in distinct times and places. Thus it might be said that each of the two paths leading away from the older approach to American religious history, that is, through a master narrative, has a role to play in Albanese's book. I explore both these paths in the remainder of this chapter before asking whether they may in fact converge. Indeed, both of these new initiatives in framing historical accounts may prove to be compatible with and possibly even derived from the older approach that they appeared to displace. But that is to leap ahead of the story.[12]

In recent decades, the topic of narratives has been intensively discussed within literary studies as well as far beyond that realm. I am not the author to provide nor is this the context in which to give a full account of that discussion. But the shadow of these exchanges has been cast across fields as diverse as general historiography, theology, and cinema studies. In this respect, the reconsideration of narrative is central to the canon-challenging and new initiative–seeking program of the last decades, so it is scarcely surprising that such discourse has come into play in the field of history writing about religion in America. Issues surrounding the nature of "narrative" became hotly contested, and extensive discussions that were taking place or were beginning to take place in other subjects suddenly became germane to writing historical accounts about religion in American society and culture. To be sure, historiography more generally was being enriched or confused, depending upon the point of view, by these same impulses. In a roundabout fashion, the fact that religious historical accounts were capable of being affected by critiques comparable to those impacting other historical subject matters was further evidence to support Henry May's proposition about the "recovery" of American religious history. But having noted these considerations, the more important next step is to review several of these proposed narrative axes.

It is convenient for my purpose that a group of students of American religion(s) dedicated several years to discussing this matter and framing a very useful analysis. Their book, *Retelling U.S. Religious History*, edited by Thomas A. Tweed, not only enlisted a group of the leading younger and middle-aged scholars but also made use of advice and counsel from some of the older and established figures.[13] Itself displaying new-style historiography, the conduct of the project exemplifies a different and far more collaborative approach to historiographical endeavors than was typical of historians working in earlier generations. So the way in which this project was conceived and executed and the conclusions it advanced deserve recognition and perhaps emulation. For our immediate purposes, however, we should note carefully the kinds of claims advanced in the volume as well as those that were rejected.

Tweed and his colleagues essentially shaped their collective effort around three motifs.[14] One is that narrative accounts are—and should be—the dominant form of history writing. Of course, these authors are all powerfully aware of the critiques that have been advanced about the unexpressed and unacknowledged particularity of most narratives. A second proposition is that the major discussions of religion in American history that were cast in narrative form, from Robert Baird's *Religion in America* to Sydney Ahlstrom's *A Religious History of the American People,* privileged a dominant Protestantism and thus worked to veil the range and degree of religious pluralism that does, and should, constitute the topic. The third proposition is that, while it would be naive to think that a single, more adequate narrative could necessarily substitute for the one they wished to discredit, some collection of alternate narratives might provide a more adequate framing of the subject. The authors offer a series of essays constructed around "sites" that might be viewed as candidates for this role.[15]

We could wish that more of those who undertake historiographical reconstruction were prepared to frame and construct their cases in as thoroughly self-conscious a way as Tweed and his colleagues did. This collection of essays deserves to be taken at face value rather than having the challenge they present blunted by raising questions about methodological niceties or comprehensiveness. Appropriating directly from their effort, we might note in this discussion some of the alternate narratives that the authors propose by way of supplementing, complementing, or supplanting a single predominating narrative account. (The comment is phrased in this way because one suspects a lack of complete unanimity among the collaborators; that is, the individuals involved might well prefer varying approaches if left on their own.)

Tweed introduced the collection with an essay entitled "Narrating U.S. Religious History."[16] Acknowledging strong examples of the preexisting tradition of narrative accounts (e.g., those showing kinship with Ahlstrom's book), Tweed emphasized that each was structured around a "foundational motif." He went on to identify some of the themes found in the literature (e.g., "the frontier," "declension and secularization," and "contest") that especially point to "identity and difference" as one theme that had proved to be frequently used in recent decades. His purpose in developing this analytical framework was to frame the alternate paths taken in some of the book's essays.

My purpose in highlighting this volume is not to subject it to scrutiny in its entirety, for instance, by dissecting each of the separate chapters and assessing them in turn. Rather, I use this carefully constructed book as an exhibit of how self-conscious attention to the construction of narrative accounts affected attempts to carry forward the historical study of religion in America. If there is a common theme to the writing, it consists of the variations rung on a complex of three related motifs, namely, "contact, boundary, and exchange."[17] In this way, Tweed and his colleagues find common analytic ground among accounts that focus on themes as divergent as sexuality (and also the active role of women) in American religion, ritual sites of various kinds, and "supply-side" perspectives. Under the latter head, for example, Roger Finke underscores the upwelling of religiously expressed effervescence in a society that lacks provision for either governing or structuring it.[18] The essays constituting the second half of the book narrate American religious materials from unusual points of view, for example, from the perspective of residents of the western lands; or of Native Americans located in the southern Appalachians; or of our northern neighbors, the Canadians. One missing topic that surely deserved to be treated as a major motif is sustained attention to race, which has been, arguably, the single most important element shaping American cultural and religious life. A final essay by Catherine Albanese concludes the book with characteristically nuanced reflections upon the phenomenon of religious exchanges across boundaries and among traditions.[19]

Another relevant project also deserves mention at this point. *New Directions in American Religious History* appeared at roughly the same time as the collection edited by Tweed.[20] Edited by Harry S. Stout and Daryl G. Hart, it too was a collaborative effort to assess the state of writing about the subject. This volume includes approximately twenty essays, most by established or senior figures, that were commissioned for a gathering held at the Wingspread Conference Center in Racine, Wisconsin, in 1993. While originating from this invitational conference, however, the published collection was less well focused than the volume produced from the project directed by Tweed.[21] Nonetheless, taken as a whole, the essays do at least implicitly address the problematic of historical narration about religious phenomena in the American past. The structure of the volume makes it evident that the central theme of a great Protestant era (which Ahlstrom believed to have ended circa 1960 with the election of John F. Kennedy or possibly in 1963 with the elevation of Pope John) still provided the fundamental axis of religious historiography about America thirty years later.[22] But the essays in the book make it equally evident that if Protestantism remained basic to America's religious complexion, it was itself fragmented, drawn into relationships with other traditions, and repeatedly in tension with other dynamic elements of America's past and present.

It would not serve the purposes of the current study to comment at length on any of the essays or on all of them in a cursory fashion. But it may be possible to delineate the implications of this volume for my effort. One of its strong dimensions is an emphasis upon region, a feature also suggested in the Tweed volume. Another dimension, less emphasized in that other group of essays, is the recognition of "stages" of development both among Protestant bodies and in American religion(s) more generally. Several authors make it evident that colonial religious practices, for example, were not replicated among all nineteenth-century Protestants, so periods within and well beyond Protestantism are manifest, and recognition of them is necessary. Incidentally, this diversification reflects the tremendous outpouring of studies about religion to which Henry May had called attention in "The Recovery of American Religious History"; of course, the appearance of his article had itself encouraged further scholarship in these materials.[23] Additional essays in the Stout and Hart volume emphasize the deep engagement with and interpenetration of religion (primarily, Protestantism) with such basic realities of American history as economic behavior, relentless urbanization, and stubborn ethnicity. Finally, several of the essays call attention to the related but independent elements of the picture such as the African American legacy, the range of Catholic traditions, and the extraordinary role played by largely secular Jewish intellectuals in the course of the twentieth century.[24] Less thoroughly integrated than the Tweed volume, the Stout and Hart collection nevertheless at once endorsed the pervasive reality of narration as the mode in which religion in American history is presented while insisting that such accounts are necessarily plural.

Taken together, these thoughtfully conceived and carefully executed collections of essays do forcefully underscore the importance of narrative accounts in presenting American religious history. Given the existence of these volumes, it is difficult to imagine that a new narrative account could be written without demonstrating sensitivity to many of the dimensions of the subject so described. The predominant role of women, trans-Pacific (as well as trans-Atlantic) immigration (not to speak of internal migrations), Native and African American cultural exchange with European settlers, religious virtuosi and their followers—all these and many other themes as well would effectively compete for requisite attention in such an undertaking. The Stout and Hart essays indicate other necessary elements in any such effort.[25]

Put in this way, however, the question necessarily before us becomes transposed. Was Sidney Ahlstrom's magisterial volume, *A Religious History of the American People*, really defective along all these axes? Ahlstrom's account did indeed implicitly allow for most of the dimensions called for in the essays that comprise Tweed's volume if we allow for the time in which it was researched and written and recognize the special interests of its author. One might almost claim that Ahlstrom's volume foreshadowed the serious attention given to the topics in the essays that make up the Stout and Hart collection. In sum, did the critique of the old narrative approach to writing historical accounts about religion in American history really establish that it was so fundamentally flawed? Or did the criticism of it really entail generational fashions more than methodological principles?[26] Even turning the question in this way suggests that only limited progress is possible, so to speak, along a path beyond Ahlstrom on the part of reformers committed to new narrative approaches. As important as self-consciousness about narrative methods may be, taken alone it is not clear that substantial progress in critical historiography is possible simply by taking this fork in the road.

Somewhat earlier, I noted two approaches that developed as means of transcending the type of narrative synthesis represented by Ahlstrom. One approach was to adopt a program to overcome the limitations in the master narrative he had embraced; this was the challenge taken up so resolutely by the collaborators in the Tweed project and in another mode and to a lesser extent at the Wingspread conference. The other approach was to recognize that religion studied through a social sciences perspective (especially in sociological literature but not excluding allied disciplines like anthropology, political science, and psychology) helped to frame generic approaches to similar subject matters in ways that permitted, indeed almost seemed to require, comparative inquiries. We have discussed one critique of the approach to religion in U.S. history in terms of an old master narrative, namely, that additional narrative lines (or themes) were required to do it justice. The other line of criticism was that tremendous insight into and understanding of religious phenomena in the United States was possible through interpreting domestic events in the light of more general social, political, and religious paradigms.[27] At a more general level, narrative accounts remain dependent upon the claim(s) their authors make that unique sequences of events uniquely provide basic insights. This alternative point of view asserts that valuable insights come through recognizing hitherto undisclosed or unobserved patterns among the behaviors humans manifest. In turn, this recognition is possible through identifying resemblances and parallels across time and space—at least as framed through theoretical perspectives. Using such paradigms permits comparative insights as well as a more dynamic view of the subjects.

The foregoing observation invites comment on the very great influence that social science disciplines have generally exercised upon historical research and writing in recent decades and in particular upon writing about religious subjects in American history. At this point, another friendly critic of Ahlstrom provides us with an opening. One of Ahlstrom's many graduate students at Yale, Peter W. Williams has gone on to a long and distinguished career at Miami University in Oxford, Ohio.[28] In his own way, Williams has ranged as widely through the history of American religion as his mentor did. Whether through collaborative efforts on encyclopedias or sustained and systematic interest in religious architecture, among other subjects, Williams has greatly enriched and expanded appreciation for Ahlstrom's subject matter. One of his earliest publications was a relatively slim volume that opened a dialogue with Ahlstrom's *A Religious History of the American People.*[29] In particular, *Popular Religion in America* took issue with the extreme commitment to the uniqueness of historical subjects that infused and directed Ahlstrom's labors. Williams, for his part and always with appreciation, suggested that resources from the social sciences might well be used to expand and deepen our understanding of the history of American religion. He had discovered in the work of Max Weber, among others, very significant insights into the tasks at hand.

Rather than develop this point by making further reference to Peter Williams's volume, we should take a somewhat broader perspective on the potential contributions available in the work of social scientists to further the historical study of American religion. I commented earlier on the role played by visitors from abroad as well as by immigrants in helping to make religion in America intelligible. Among that group, a figure like Alexis de Tocqueville certainly stands out (although, as suggested, a not insignificant school of opinion might give honor of place to Philip Schaff). Tocqueville stands for a broader tradition of social theorizing, however, that had its roots in predecessors like Montesquieu; later, this tradition was elaborated more fully by Emil Durkheim and his successors.[30] In the works of these theorists of society, religion played a very significant role, linked as deeply as they thought it was to the existence of communities. It provided the coherence that held them together and finally made possible their long-term viability. A different though related strand of thought, associated most fully with Max Weber and best known through his association of the Protestant ethic with the spirit of capitalism, placed more emphasis on the analysis of social dynamics but also insisted upon the noteworthy contribution of religion to the existence of societies.[31] Taken together, by the middle of the twentieth century these strands had been woven into a fabric of thought that exercised a powerful influence on historiography in general and writing about religious history in particular in the United States. Among those associated with this continuing social sciences influence upon historiography are names such as Clifford Geertz, Robert Bellah, Anthony Wallace, Edward Shils, Mary Douglas, and Peter Berger, to name only a very few individuals, and of that group a number remain active as scholars.[32] Many others who made significant contributions, for example, Talcott Parsons of an earlier generation, were also instrumental in the development of this powerful and influential period in the analysis of societies and their dynamics.[33]

In the present chapter it is less important for several reasons to attribute particular theories or insights to specific individuals than it is to sketch the manner and degree of influence that flowed from their collective efforts. One reason is that there will be occasion to return to comment further and in some detail on the work of at least several of these scholars in the concluding chapter. Without this school of thought and the resources it has made available to us, it would be difficult to identify and analyze a basic question, namely, how to discuss the religious sentiments that attach to America as in our purported "civil religion." Certain of these figures will be reintroduced as the more general topic of an American religion receives attention. The other reason to treat them as a group rather than individually in the present context is that their direct influence on historical writing about religion in America came through appropriation by others of specific concepts more than by formal recasting of historiographical procedures.[34] Calling attention to two examples of paradigms that drew deeply upon and developed from this broad tradition of social thought will make this point. One was a relatively condensed proposal to model a particular class of social interactions, namely, those encompassed by the term *revitalization movement;* the other was a much more generalized observation about social orders, namely, the interplay in political regimes between center and periphery that describes and analyzes cultural relationships more generally.

The concept of a revitalization movement as a specific mechanism in human societies can be traced to the work of Anthony F. C. Wallace, who defined it as such in an article published many decades ago.[35] At root, he was concerned to frame an understanding of how a weaker culture (in his instant case, the Native American) made use of its cultural heritage to construct grounds for resisting a stronger culture (the majority or imperial American) that was bearing down upon it. Of course, the revitalization movement was a work of imagination articulated by a prophetic figure who called forth from his people what was, in fact if not in name, a newly refashioned and usually selective version of the older challenged traditions. Rather than suffer deterioration and collapse in the face of overwhelming political and social pressure, the reconstructed culture generated a new idiom with which to survive, holding forth the promise that the people might again flourish. The concept of a revitalization movement—a model for one kind of social interaction—found ready acceptance among anthropologists. In terms of appreciation for the inventiveness of cultures, this concept proved to be readily applicable to phenomena such as millenarian movements arising among tribes in contemporaneous Indonesia interacting with Westerners as well as similar episodes among Native Americans resisting an aggressive and overpowering majority culture. Such applications of the concept seemed to be direct and unproblematic.[36]

But the idea of a revitalization movement, if slightly broadened, can also help to structure an interpretation of phenomena like revivalism and religious awakenings, which have been widely present in U.S. religious history. Indeed, William

McLoughlin, longtime historian at Brown who was widely respected for his detailed studies of church and state in colonial New England as well as for chronicling the fate of the Cherokee nation, made such a direct application of the concept. In a relatively slight monograph entitled *Revivals, Awakenings, and Reform,* he crafted a bold proposal that identified a series of great awakenings as the spine of American history that gave order to political eras and periods of social reform.[37] The details of his case are less important for us than the example it offers of an established and respected historian, thoroughly committed to interpreting the uniqueness of singular events or series of events, who found in this model a means to illuminate the broader reaches of American history. It is especially interesting that a recent Nobel Prize winner in economics has proposed a roughly comparable framework for understanding the long-term political dynamics of American society.[38]

How exactly does the paradigm of the revitalization movement work to assist the historian? As a schematic understanding of a special kind of social or cultural exchange, this concept directs the interpreter to certain basic relationships. For one, it suggests that attention should be directed to cultural interactions and, more particularly, that one cultural group may (for whatever reason) feel challenged or adversely impacted by another group. For another, it suggests that some "translation" will occur; namely, the threat experienced in one mode or dimension of human life may be counteracted through response in and through another. Finally, it suggests that rather than focus primarily on a particular prophet or singular religious leader, attention should be given to the dynamic movement that makes possible, while also constraining, his or her actions. In sum, the model of the revitalization movement instructs the historian about kinds of promising questions that might be asked, data that might be gathered, or inquiries that should be made to comprehend or analyze particular events.[39]

For another illustration of how social scientific perspectives have become important to historians in general and to students of religion in particular, I briefly turn to the concept of center and periphery as a very broadly used analytic perspective on a range of subjects. The particular formulation is associated with Edward Shils, and it probably entails a necessarily strong association with political perspectives.[40] But it also serves as a valuable means of orienting attention to specifically religious problematics. The most direct application is surely its congruence with a traditional society such as we know in Europe. There the existence of an established church directly mirrors political dynamics, at once reinforcing the regime by investing it with authority while at the same time drawing power and influence from that political reality. If association with the center is obvious, the role of periphery (cultural and spatial) in making a place for sectarian activity is equally manifest. In a less highly structured society, such as that represented in the early American republic, the absence of a clear center correlated with religious disestablishment. As a denominational society, nineteenth- and twentieth-century

America had no highly structured or manifestly institutional-ized religious core, although I necessarily return to this subject in the last chapter.[41] This does not mean, however, that activi-ties associated with the periphery are absent. On the contrary, we have learned that religious innovation and effervescence may flourish where there is no strong center. Indeed, the ab-sence of a strong center may help to frame the unprecedented level of diverse religious activity that has characterized American society.

Among sociologists, Peter Berger in his early work iden-tified this notion of the intensity of religious innovation at the margins of American society as a salient feature.[42] An emphasis on activities at the periphery is entirely consistent with the thinking of economists who look to the margin to find the changes that leverage the whole society. Roger Finke and Rodney Stark have carried this line of thinking furthest with respect to religious phenomena.[43] Many religious histo-rians received their book, *The Churching of America, 1776– 1990*, as a presumptuous and unsophisticated rendering of historical materials, claiming the authors were ill informed about the previous uses of their purportedly new data and the interpretation to which they had already been subjected. This criticism is surely warranted. In another perspective, however, the study did recognize the immensely important role of in-novation and inspiration in explicating the quite extraordi-nary pattern of successes and declines among religious bodies in America. My judgment stops short of attempting to "explain" the quite extraordinary pattern of American experience out of respect for historians' skepticism about Finke and Stark's supply-side model of religion in American history. But the basic point has already been made, namely, the important role that can be played by an orienting concept like center and periphery even if it does not entail the almost mechanistic features of a template or model like that provided by the concept of revitalization movements.[44]

Two additional observations are appropriate in summing up this brief discussion of how social scientific thought has affected historical studies of American religion in the course of the last decades. One is simply that the influence has been very great indeed. Even historians who are in principle opposed to the incorporation of concepts and devices from this particular source find themselves making use of terminology and concepts that have developed particular significance in the social sciences.[45] While they may resist the full application of such resources in a technical manner, historians' use of them in ordinary ways at some level endows them with at least subliminal influence upon the latter's work. Of course, many of the references and comments already offered make it plain that numerous historians readily embrace in a more technical way the insights and understandings that derive from this source. Anthropology has "thickened up" historiography to its benefit.[46] A second observation follows hard on the first. It is that however powerful the influence of social scientific thinking on historiography in general or the historiography of religion in America in particular, the fundamental use of narration to construct such accounts has not been challenged.[47] The earlier example of William McLoughlin's use of revitalization theory to construct an overall account of American religion illustrates this point.

Where does this leave us at the end of this chapter? In my opinion, the last several decades of historical writing about religion in American history have been extremely rich and have manifested great inventiveness. If the effort has been made, post-Ahlstrom, to push beyond simple narration to multiple narratives, that has served more to reinforce than to challenge the premise that a diverse and compelling subject matter is available to those specializing in these materials. Both the general stimulation and the particular paradigms available from social scientific thought have impacted directly as well as indirectly on work in the field. This has also served to validate the enterprise, perhaps even to bring endorsement from unexpected quarters. Certainly, one direct outcome has been to elevate the importance of comparative studies.[48] A necessary comment is surely also appropriate at this point to the effect that at least two strategies for comparison are possible. One is first-order, in which several societies are inspected in parallel. A favorite point of comparison in the New World is that between the United States and Canada, although it might be useful as a matter of course to expect that Mexico would be part of that set as well. Such an effort has not yet been systematically attempted, to my knowledge.[49] But there is another kind of comparison—we might term it second-order—in which theoretical constructs are used to explore similarities as well as differences in light of recognized dynamics or patterns that seem to be relatively common. In concluding this chapter, I might make the simple comment that, to date, historiographical interpretation of religion in America has certainly made less use of this kind of directed application of social science work than is possible and likely less than will seem desirable in a longer-term perspective.

RELIGION(S)
OF AMERICA

From Civil Religion to Milling at the Mall

IN THE INITIAL CHAPTER of this book, I traced the development of interest in the historiography of religion in the United States, emphasizing its origins in the nineteenth century and proposing that it culminated in a well-recognized field of study for which Sydney Ahlstrom's *A Religious History of the American People* could stand as a marker. In the second chapter, I noted that Henry May's essay "The Recovery of American Religious History" could also serve much the same purpose of marking a transition point, albeit through charting a different and ascendant strand of historiography. This led me to review two kinds of challenges to singular narrative accounts of the subject. One is the argument that the pluralism of religious phenomena in America makes it imperative to make use of multiple accounts, while the other is the initiative to make extensive use of paradigms that derive from the flourishing social sciences to enlarge our understanding of the subject. In making this case, it is appropriate to invoke one more figure whose profile does not stand as high among those concerned to interpret American religious history as it deserves to. Marcus Lee Hansen held the promise of becoming the first great historian of immigration to America. Details of his life and career are not known to me, but he seems to have completed only the first volume of what was projected to be a multivolume study of that subject.[1] Indeed, written in the interwar decades of the twentieth century, *The Atlantic Migration* laid the groundwork for the subsequent scholarship that has extended critical discussion of immigration to our time as well as attending to additional sources of large-scale immigration from Africa and Asia.[2]

Immigration and its consequences are necessarily a topic of immense importance in understanding America and perhaps especially the religious dimensions of American history. Hansen recognized that migration sets up cultural dynamics that have extraordinary consequences for societies so impacted. Why does the name of Marcus Lee Hansen deserve mention at this point? Primarily because as a historian working in the 1920s and 1930s he could have, with very little "prep time," so to speak, stepped into our contemporary discussions. In his own way, while endorsing the framework of a master narrative, he nonetheless emphasized the importance of searching out the alternate narratives as well through opening the door to study of particular communities before their residence in America as well as in the transit they made to this land and in their settlement in it.[3] Hansen also understood the kinds of models social scientists have helped us to adopt. In particular, he developed reflections about the cultural by-products of immigration. In a wonderful essay, "Immigration and Puritanism," he asked why it was that the Puritans cast such a long shadow over American history (which is, of course, a major question lurking beneath the surface of this work).[4]

Hansen's answer to this rhetorical question was not to marshal arguments framed along predictable lines. Among them might have been (to reach for more contemporary versions of his point) that the gene pool of the Puritans was dominant or that it was by means of political domination that the Puritans secured a hegemony that would last through several centuries. Rather, he proposed that the Puritans exercised decisive and continuing influence in and through American history and historiography because, as the first of many concentrated immigrations, they worked through the cultural strategies for survival and eventual success that succeeding generations of immigrants, coming to America from markedly different points of origin, have rediscovered as the key to their successes in the new world of American society.[5] Indeed, such a framing of the issue, which Hansen proposed in the 1930s, is entirely congruent with the broad historiographical preoccupations of the last half of the twentieth century. Citing Marcus Lee

Hansen in this manner suggests that already, well before World War II, a historian had reached the essential grounds that recent generations have achieved in the way that has been suggested in these chapters.

I ended the discussion in chapter 2 by proposing that, while challenges had served to enlarge and deepen the interpretation of religion in American history, they had not fundamentally redefined the endeavor. This leads directly to consideration of another dimension of the overall subject, namely, whether it is necessary to recognize that the American nation might itself become a religious object. If this is the case, the question follows, How might we examine this topic? Thus the title of this chapter, "Religion(s) of America," to which I have added the subtitle "From Civil Religion to Milling at the Mall." Hansen's work is also a bridge to the concluding chapter of this volume. As we shall see, his "three generation hypothesis"—"What the son wishes to forget, the grandson wishes to remember"—links directly to the subject of this last chapter, namely, proposals concerning the religion(s) of America.[6]

I begin this discussion with reference to an author of note whose work proved to be of great symbolic importance, highly instrumental in shaping the study of religion in America. This is Will Herberg, a marvelously storied figure who moved from secular left-wing labor organizer in the 1930s, to appreciative confidant of Reinhold Niebuhr and theologian of Jewish traditions in the 1940s and 1950s, and then to faculty member at Drew University in the 1960s and 1970s while migrating politically in a decidedly conservative direction. In 1960, Herberg published a study entitled *Protestant-Catholic-Jew* that was interesting at several levels.[7] In the simplest terms, it was the assertion that post–World War II America had come of age as a religiously pluralistic society. Comprised of equal parts anecdotes and incidental data, the volume argued that religion was critical to American society and prominent within it as a means of conferring identity. And, like any other commodity, brands counted. Most specifically, there were three main brands of religion recognized by Americans, the three traditions of Herberg's title. At another, more complex level, Herberg asserted with equal assurance that these brands (and there was no reason why there should be only three) were but varietal expressions of a more substantial and fundamental reality, namely, the American Way of Life. This cultural reality he took to be the real "content" of the three traditions of his title. In one of its guises, the book was a prophetic critique of the shallowness of traditional religions as practiced in the United States, for Herberg saw them as at root expressing a thinly disguised American patriotism or even boosterism.[8]

How and why did Herberg reach this conclusion? His basic insight was to propose that several dynamics were at work in American society and that these had come together to elevate the importance of religion in making it possible for the society to function. He directly appropriated, for example, the strand of social theorizing developed by David Reisman and his collaborators, who had proposed that a sense of identity was a means of establishing social location and that a sense of social location was critical for Americans in the mid–twentieth century.[9] He also attempted to make use of (through generalizing from it) Hansen's three generation hypothesis. Hansen had observed transgenerational changes in Lutheranism. Herberg proposed that the dynamics Hansen observed were in fact a basic mechanism in American society. By this means, he thought, the particularities of first-generation immigrants—codes of dress, languages, folk customs, diets, to name some basic elements of ethnicity—were metamorphosed into more generic and possibly interchangeable "religious brands" by the third generation of residence in America, namely, the Protestantism, Catholicism, and Judaism of Herberg's title.[10] To express his idea in somewhat different terms, Herberg took ethnicities to be the intermediate forms taken by immigrant cultures as they resided in and adapted to the United States. These ethnicities also at once support and sustain communities that define themselves primarily through religious differences because, in the American context, religious particularities are understood not to threaten the social order.[11]

There are two major observations about Herberg's provocative work that should be offered in the context of this discussion. The first is that he deserves credit for explicitly addressing the challenge of trying to explain the prominence of religion in American society, a feature that makes the United States stand out in marked contrast to other highly modern societies.[12] He did this by identifying dynamic cultural patterns, perhaps best characterized as "mechanisms," that make it plausible to think that the social function of religion is deeply rooted in this nation's experience. Religion does something in America that is perhaps not strictly paralleled elsewhere, and thus it has a social utility that has conferred special cultural importance upon it in the American context.[13]

Several evaluative comments about *Protestant-Catholic-Jew* are appropriate at this point. One is simply that, when we allow for advances in the data gathering and social theorizing, Herberg's use of ethnicity and its relationship to immigration has stood the test of time remarkably well, offering a historiographic means of identifying and describing certain dynamics of American society. A second is that he did not claim that other parallel mechanisms might not be needed to explain the phenomena in a fuller way either for the past or the future.[14] In short, his approach in principle would allow the use of additional models or mechanisms to sustain his basic point, which was that religion plays a very special and significant role in American society.

The second major observation is that Herberg approached, if he did not reach, the point of insisting that, understood in this fashion, American society entailed a kind of commitment to it on the part of its members that should be analytically understood in "religious" terms. Insofar as the American Way of Life was the core spiritual substance of the denominational religions, it was to be understood as a quasi religion that made the nation itself an object for the religious affections and commitments of its citizens. Herberg actually expounded at some length on this point and used the term "civic religion" to identify this phenomenon. For him it was a truer way of comprehending in the American context what most called patriotism.[15] He also recognized that this concept reached back at least to the insight of Rousseau, who had thought such a means of attachment to the polis (or political society) was critical. Of course, this notion in turn derived from classical antiquity, when loyalty to Rome, signaled through deference to the divine emperor, provided the social and cultural glue for a great pluralistic empire.[16]

While he did not make much of it, Herberg also recognized that this line of thought was consonant with the theorizing undertaken by Emile Durkheim about the place of religion in social systems. Religion becomes, so to speak, an idiom in which a society presents an image of itself to its consciousness, thereby projecting and conferring on itself a cosmic significance. While Durkheim worked through his ideas literally in an armchair, theorizing about Australian aborigines and their totems, the possibility of applying these perspectives to more modern and perhaps more complex social groups became readily apparent.[17] Herberg understood this but may have been inhibited by his own deep attachment to the strains of prophecy in the traditions with which he specially identified (Jewish Torah and Christian Old Testament). If the three traditions of his title were reduced to manifestations of a deeper and shared American Way of Life, his personal instincts were to criticize that object as shallow and unworthy of true devotion.[18] In these terms, no better case could be made for the authenticity of a civic religion of Americanism. So Herberg's analysis broke off on an equivocal note. He affirmed the significance and inevitability of a self-referential religion centered on America while yet also believing that it was unworthy of allegiance on the part of those humans whose consciences might have been tutored by the ancient prophets.[19]

Within a decade of his writing *Protestant-Catholic-Jew,* the subject I have been considering in terms of the "outer limits" of Will Herberg's analysis of American society moved to center stage. The name was slightly changed, for the phenomenon was termed "civil religion" instead of "civic religion," and the attitude toward or valuation of such a concept had reversed 180 degrees. If, to speak in terms of direct contrasts, Will Herberg had been driven to reflect on the subject by the logic of his line of inquiry, Robert Bellah viewed the topic in idealistic terms, deeming it worthy of respect and sensitive appropriation.[20] What happened to bring about this change in valuation? A compound reference may suffice to indicate why: internationally, the military involvement of America in a war in Southeast Asia and, domestically, the antiwar (or anticonscription) movement. In his influential essay, Bellah portrayed a better America that dissident youth could affirm and love even as they resisted both military service and the broader war effort that required it of them.

It must be said that, at least implicitly, Bellah developed a rather fuller version of American civil religion than Herberg had done for civic faith. Bellah articulated a range of references to the nation's past that came together in a plausible religious structure.[21] Ideologically, this nation, the last great hope of the earth, was birthed with the ideal of freedom for all. A series of leaders then exemplified this high mission in human history. In retrospect, they had been elevated to semidivine status. Many of them were presidents, like Washington, Lincoln, the Roosevelts, and Kennedy, but others were without the distinction of that office, for example, Martin Luther King Jr. The calendar of national holidays structured time so as to make the sacred events of the community real to its members. Sacred sites as varied as Bunker Hill, Gettysburg, the Alamo, and local burial grounds formed tangible places where the past could be revisited and relived, affirmed and embraced. Activities as mundane as making trips to the post office or as high toned as grieving over an assassinated president bound Americans to America.

Bellah's piece was suggestive more than exhaustive, its references were partial rather than full, and its implications were not entirely explicated. But the response to his ideas was extraordinary, and he became something of an overnight celebrity. The professor of sociology became preacher to the protestors, pastor to the expatriates, and prophet to those resisting the government's policy. It is difficult to imagine that any other *Daedalus* piece has evoked anything like the response that attended this one, or at least the kind of response represented in its approbation. It would be possible (and fun at least for those who follow this topic) to chart the development of the exchanges that followed in countless conferences, in products of all kinds and shapes from the presses, and at the local equivalents of Hyde Park. The civil religion discussion moved along several axes. One axis was certainly a moral critique of the war. Another axis explored the adequacy of this construct as a means through which to analyze the phenomenon of citizens' attachment to the nation under stress in terms that construed it as a particular religion. A third axis entailed disagreement about whether civil religion manifested continuing historical reality.[22]

It is tempting to revisit these questions at greater length than is possible in this context. It is important to note, however, that in the end the extensive discussions seemed to be inconclusive on these matters. Certainly, individual studies did take off from the topic to explore subject areas in far more adequate fashion; substantial literature on sacred sites and the phenomenon of public commemoration has continued to be produced through the succeeding decades.[23] An example of a recently created site would be the Holocaust Memorial in Washington, D.C. At the level of theory and construct, however, these exchanges did not move the discussion much further along. With respect to its usefulness, some efforts were made to underline the broader reality of related phenomena and perhaps even the existence of developed civil religion(s) in other societies around the globe. But little of such scholarship played back and informed the shaping of historiography about religion in America.

At least for some, the most interesting questions had to do with whether the phenomenon had a continuing existence. Bellah had himself characterized civil religion as "elaborate and well-institutionalized."[24] The more useful question to pose is whether, while the relevant elements associated with civil religion, like observances and attitudes, may in fact exist across time, it is not more likely that their confluence into a full-orbed religion is periodic, increasing in importance in response to particular stimuli or receding in times of relative social tranquility. Such a perspective would allow for the possibility that a fully developed civil religion of America exists only episodically and under very particular circumstances, for example, when the American nation faces threats to its existence.[25] To interpret civil religion as episodic would allow for the fullest attention to its elements while explaining the absence of continuing manifestations of fully developed civil religion. It would be useful to attempt to develop a summary assessment of this kind, but that exercise would distort the framework of this study.

What we should take away from this brief recollection of the civil religion discussion is twofold. On the one hand, it presupposed and thus brought to more general attention a theoretical literature that undergirded the concept that America might exist through its collective representation of itself. This is another, although surely related, dimension of the search in which we have been engaged for religion(s) in American history because it postulates that alongside and underneath the particular religions there may well be a religion centered on the whole society or nation. On the other hand, recalling the civil religion exchanges opens the door to asking whether less condensed and more diffused means of attachment to the collective society may exist that link Americans in whole or in part to the nation. As this line of questioning has been pursued, it is increasingly disconnected from the civil religion question. This subject is worth discussing in itself, however, and also in terms of whether the extended civil religion exchanges can provide a useful perspective on these subsequent proposals.

Initially, we should turn to the first branch of the question, that is, whether a religion of America may not underlie and suffuse itself through many if not all particular manifold expressions of religion in America. Of course, Bellah's development of the idea of civil religion was not the first to propose such, any more than credit for originating it belongs to Herberg with his earlier notion of civic faith. Taken as an intellectual construct, this notion properly traces back through William James and before him Walt Whitman, at least to Ralph Waldo Emerson.[26] No one of the foregoing pursued this insight with the relentless rigor and energy, however, that Harold Bloom brought to the subject in his book *The American Religion,* published in 1992.[27] Adopting the persona of a religious critic, Bloom relentlessly traced the emergence of what he took to be a peculiarly American creed. He argued that, at its core, the American religion posits that the solitary individual is free to find God, or the divine, in himself or herself. Bloom's formulation is instructive: "The American finds God in herself or himself, but only after finding the freedom to know God by experiencing total inward solitude. Freedom, in a very special sense, is the preparation without which God will not allow himself to be revealed in the self. And this freedom is in itself double; the spark or spirit must know itself to be free both of other selves and of the created world. In perfect solitude, the American spirit learns again its absolute isolation as a spark of God floating in a sea of space."[28]

Such a formulation, and in particular its capsule expression as "a spark of God floating in a sea of space," is essentially Gnostic.[29] Bloom himself readily confesses to such a self-understanding. From this vantage point, he has deconstructed the traditional claims of the Judaism of the rabbis as well as the Christianities of both priests and preachers. Of course, Gnosticism has its own history. To identify such a hyperindividualistic religious position as Gnosticism is noteworthy primarily because in the case of modern America it is a phenomenon of the masses rather than an intellectual option primarily embraced by the few or among a restricted set of members who understand themselves to be members of an elite. So Bloom's "American religion" is something we might term a "democratic Gnosticism," the likes of which, he thinks, is new under the sun.

Where do we find this gospel? For Bloom it is hidden "in, with, and under" the conventional religious attachments of the society. His chief exhibits, namely, the Mormon movement and the Southern Baptist Convention, turn out to run against the expected grain.[30] But to overemphasize these particular groups would be willfully to mislead, because Bloom finds Gnosticism for the masses implicit in virtually all creeds and confessions. It is the fundamental strand of the African American religious experience no less than of the Christian Scientists; it lurks within the heart of the high traditions, episcopal of whatever stripe, and resides among their resistors too, like Presbyterians and members of Jewish groups. So Bloom finds the American religion in virtually every nook and corner of the society.

When did it come into being? If we seek to locate a decisive event as its founding moment, Bloom proposes Cane Ridge, that first great manifestation of revivalism at the beginning of the nineteenth century.[31] At once condensing and fusing the individual's simultaneous experience of solitude and discovery of self, this new mass spiritual possibility became the characteristic American mode of being religious. From such a point of view, the great varieties of religious expression in the United States, from the arcane theologizing of Joseph Smith Jr. to the unmasked television pentecostal promisers of recent decades like Jim Bakker, in essence convey the same message: redemption comes from embracing individual solitude, at once finding God and self as the center and periphery of the cosmos.

From this critical perspective, Bloom's American religion is both little differentiated as a religion and seemingly without attachment to a social matrix.[32] It is so essentialized that individual details, indeed, historical episodes, recede from view or dissolve into insignificance. While offering a powerful insight into the common culture of American society, religion defined in so desiccated a fashion loses its explanatory power and its significance for those interpreting it. It is not altogether persuasive that this kind of Gnosticism for the hoi polloi could have attached to and energized great causes that entailed sacrifice and loss. Challenging examples include those who at great cost defend a way of life that entails slavery in the nineteenth century or a nation of loosely tied regions committing to a war to vanquish the Axis powers in the twentieth. Thus we are faced with radical alternatives: either Harold Bloom's proposal regarding the American religion really means that there is no American community or nation, or his Gnostic construct helps us only marginally in our quest to understand it.

In trying to explain why this is so, it may be useful to observe that Bloom's religious criticism by both intent and design emphasizes one dimension of religion to the virtual exclusion of another. There can be no question that the experience of ecstasy—standing outside of, or transcending, the self as constituted in daily life—is central to religion and helps to define its core.[33] Without at least the illusion of self-transcendence there is no religion. But there is also a no less critical component of religion, at least in the view that seems

defensible, and this is that any ecstatic moments essential to
the definition of religion are related to specific communities,
whether they are located in space and time or function in the
imagination. It is the dialectical relationship between ecstasy
and community that defines the presence of religion.[34] In these
terms, it is clear that Gnostic ecstasy as an intellectual exercise
does not require community and that without relationship to
a social matrix such an embrace of self is at most "borderline
religion." That Gnosticism has been a generalized phenomenon in human history, at least in the West, would seem to be
overwhelming evidence for that contention. In these terms,
the critical issue that faces anyone searching for manifest-
ation(s) of an American religion becomes the times, sites, and
circumstances under which the experience of ecstasy attaches
to the American community.

   One example of the experience of ecstasy attaching to the
American community is in episodes that have been identified
with civil religion. We recall the spontaneous outpourings of
grief at the assassination of—or even the attempted assassination of—a sitting president (in the one case, JFK, in the
other, Ronald Reagan). The collective expressions of solidarity
with victims (and others who suffered) after the terrorist attacks of September 11, 2001, were a comparable episode. But
these are grand kinds of examples, and we need to identify
simpler instances if there is to be a serious case made for the
significance of a religion of America or religion of the American nation. With Will Herberg and Robert Bellah, we might

think that the denominations and religious groups of the society do carry an American religion "in, with, and under" their symbols, ceremonies, and creeds. But it also seems right to think that certain elements stand free of conventional religious bodies and exist on their own. Possibly the first systematic student of these matters was W. Lloyd Warner, whose extensive five-volume *Yankee City Series* explicitly applied Durkheimian models to American society.[35] Studying Newburyport, Massachusetts, Warner found something like structured occasions for inducing ecstasy-in-community in the American context in numerous diverse locations that ranged from the town's celebration of Memorial Day to the functioning of its political parties at the local level.

Warner's fieldwork was done in the 1930s, and if we ask what other kinds of inquiry he might have made in more recent decades, the list would include at least the following in addition to more recent examples of the explicit community events and political processes that he charted: the place and role of the media, the recasting and relocation of the workplace, the alternate activities of leisure time, and the reshaping of consumption. Many will respond to these suggestions by thinking that these sites of cultural activity that might embody religious significance are not as distinct and separate as the list implies. Indeed, it is not clear that Lloyd Warner would have seen them as so distinct from each other, for he pioneered the analysis of symbol structures that, while cutting across aspects of ordinary life, concurrently function to unify our experience of it. His analysis of the then-recent radio soap opera as a strand of American self-understanding would do as well as an approach to delineating the real cultural significance of the television soaps at the end of the twentieth century.[36] But the basic point is to identify some of the dimensions of American society that embody cultural codes that carry the American religion as much as the manifestly religious and political dimensions do and whose role in so doing has been widely commented upon. In the interests of respecting the format of this book, I comment on only the first and last items of the above list: the media and patterns of consumption.

Warner's analysis of radio soaps suggests that the media, which have developed so rapidly in the last half-century, represent one location in which we should look for evidence of a religion focused on America. At the outset of the twenty-first century, the contemporary American media comprise a virtually seamless web, encompassing not only modern versions of early forms of community expression and consciousness such as newspapers and both voluntary and political gatherings but also later forms of entertainment such as plays and films.[37] Most significantly, the earlier lines of demarcation between news and opinion have largely dissolved or eroded. For our world, sports as spectacle is melded with both news as entertainment and sitcom as cultural commentary, and the composite becomes a constraining social template for American life. Furthermore, advertising has insinuated itself into the presentation of culture, and culture is cannibalized into advertising. The whole complex is an extraordinary evocation of the American Way of Life, at once reminiscent of while dramatically exceeding Will Herberg's vision of that complex as the spiritual structure of the society.

No less does the economic model of a society oriented toward consumption stand as an American achievement. David M. Potter wrote a wonderful book many decades ago entitled *People of Plenty* in which he explored the refocusing of the economy on consumption as the key to understanding American culture.[38] What had been a basically regionalized economy before World War II has become a nationalized, even internationalized, structure as we enter the twenty-first century. Farming, like merchandising, has become the domain of specialized operations that span the continent and threaten to take on the world. Particular beers, brands of autos, styles of clothing (male as well as female), packaged foods, to suggest only a few of the products catering to the most basic human needs, have all been recast in reality and in our consciousness through the force of advertising in order to provide templates for our lives as Americans. While the internationalizing of this economy may seem to undercut the claim that it is centered on America, considered as a spiritual structure for living it is indelibly and ineradicably American. We might observe that globalization comprises the American form of imperialism.

Harold Bloom's Gnostic content may describe the intellectuals' means of comprehending the American religion. But the line of argument taken in this chapter is to insist that, except in the most esoteric forms of its expression, reference to the American community is there, thoroughly embedded within the culture and not removed or remote from it. In this sense, "milling at the mall," to which my subtitle refers, is a kind of temple-work of the American religion. The mall is a clear reference to the social location where the brands that most powerfully carry this spiritual possibility are assembled. The milling aspect reminds us that, however transitory and superficial the community that gathers at the mall, it is the site where we see others—and are seen by others—engaging in common acts. Of course, with the explosion of mail-order catalogs and purchases through telephone- and Internet-based ordering systems, our society has invented virtual malls and imagined communities to an extent that few would have deemed feasible until very recently.[39] But are the religious functions and symbolic contents of the activities so very different from attendance at the parish churches or constrained participation in dissenting conventicles in earlier ages?

Accordingly, if this study moves toward a conclusion, it is that American society at the beginning of the twenty-first century embodies a cultural life that includes a spiritual or religious dimension. This is to say, America operates in terms of a set of assumptions through which the cosmos is regularized and explained and that offers an instrumental means of engaging with it. At the same time, as a society, America has permitted Old World religious traditions as well as new spiritual initiatives the space for a flourishing life. For this the most modern of nations to prove to be so hospitable to ancient preoccupations and traditions is remarkable. If nothing else, it has made those easy assumptions about the inevitability of secularization, taken for granted by several generations of intellectuals in the last century, seem disconnected from the gritty and grainy world we actually inhabit. Most of all, it suggests that we need to understand more adequately this mysterious phenomenon—religion. For moderns as well as peoples of ancient times, religion entails a kind of power that we are not well prepared to comprehend. As we reflect upon a world in which terrorism draws its recruits and frames its causes in religious terms, understanding it becomes a special—and a necessary—burden. This task takes us beyond our review of the categories that have shaped and sharpened historiographical inquiry, but it is consistent with that challenge to foster a critically informed analysis of religion and the American nation.

NOTES

Introduction

1. Sidney Mead's contribution as a historian of American religion is discussed in the first chapter. He was the first specialist in American religious history to focus his interpretation of the United States, religiously considered, directly on the issue of American exceptionalism. He rested that claim on his interpretations of the founders and the founding documents. The claim is, of course, sufficiently protean that it has assumed many different shapes and carries varying significances.

2. An expansive claim was advanced by Seymour M. Lipset, namely that America was the initial "new nation," providing a template for numerous comparable new nations that have been founded since World War II. See *The First New Nation* (New York: Basic Books, 1963). It is noteworthy that Lipset emphasized the importance of religion in the shaping of the new American nation (and implicitly other new nations) in the absence of the traditional social bases of nations formed in the "old style."

3. This point—that the inquiry neglects important authors—is painfully obvious. As one example, Edwin S. Gaustad has been a major figure in the field for the last half century and has published a full range of studies about religion in American history, including several noteworthy monographs, a comprehensive narrative account, and a very influential historical atlas, recently reissued in a substantially revised version. Daniel Dorchester, a major author from the second half of the nineteenth century,

does not appear in the discussion either. Both of these figures and many others currently alive as well as many now deceased would necessarily populate an inclusive narrative account of the field's development.

1. Religion in America

1. *Democracy in America* has recently, and deservedly, received scholarly attention, including several new editions incorporating new translations. Tracing Tocqueville's commentary about the significance of religion in the slices of American life he observed was part of the appreciation many generations developed for his insights into developing American society.

2. Henry Reeve's translation, which made the book available for American readers, was first published in 1838 (New York: Dearborn and Co.). It has provided the usual reference point for use of Tocqueville's observations on American society.

3. John Noonan announced his "discovery" of an "unpublished account" by a sister, "Angelique." He reports her (purported) reflections on the subject of religion in the new United States, implicitly endorsing Americans' superior grasp of the subject (in comparison to her brother's). See John T. Noonan Jr., "The Foremost of Political Institutions," in *The Lustre of Our Country* (Berkeley: University of California Press, 1998), 95–115.

4. Perry Miller's judgment that Philip Schaff had superior insight into the special characteristics and significance that religion had developed in the United States led to his republishing Schaff's several lectures; see Philip Schaff, *America: A Sketch of Its Political, Social, and Religious Character*, ed. Perry Miller (Cambridge, Mass.: Belknap Press, 1961). See note 12.

5. Perry Miller's monumental scholarship and writing about the Puritans kindled academic interest in the subject in the middle decades of the twentieth century and inspired the extensive work

of a generation of scholars on that subject. See, especially, *The New England Mind*, vol. 1 (Cambridge, Mass.: Harvard University Press, 1939; reprint, 1954) and a set of influential essays, *Errand into the Wilderness* (Cambridge, Mass.: Harvard University Press, 1956). Others in Miller's generation also contributed to study of the topic, although among American scholars the discussion of trans-Atlantic Puritanism's relationship to the subsequent development of the United States tended to take off from Miller's arresting scholarship. Even his most insistent critics did not disagree with the emphasis he gave to the significance of the Puritans' biblically rooted self-understanding for the construction of their ideology. In this sense, the beginnings of critical historiography about American self-understanding should not be retrojected wholesale into the Colonial period. It certainly is evident, however, that there were continuities in the symbols as well as resemblances in the teleological frameworks that carried over into the rise of critical historiography that is the subject of this chapter.

6. Peter Gay, *A Loss of Mastery: Puritan Historians in Colonial America* (Berkeley: University of California Press, 1966).

7. An appropriate example is Cotton Mather, whose *Magnalia Christi Americana*, published in 1702, located events in the New World in terms of their fulfillment of ancient prototypes. See Sacvan Bercovitch, *The Puritan Origins of the American Self* (New Haven, Conn.: Yale University Press, 1975).

8. Adams has been highlighted as an early example of how a few women dedicated tremendous energy and initiative to intellectual undertakings. Both Sydney Ahlstrom and the volume edited by Thomas Tweed acknowledge Adams's labors but point to her idiosyncrasies (see references to these volumes below).

9. Henry Warner Bowden dedicated several books to studying the rise of church historiography and its relationship to general historiography. See, especially, *Church History in the Age of*

Science: Historiographical Patterns in the United States, 1876–1918 (Chapel Hill: University of North Carolina Press, 1971) and *Church History in an Age of Uncertainty: Historiographical Patterns in the United States, 1906–1990* (Carbondale: Southern Illinois University Press, 1991). See also Henry Warner Bowden, ed., *A Century of Church History: The Legacy of Philip Schaff* (Carbondale: Southern Illinois University Press, 1988).

10. Baird's volume appeared in its first American edition in 1856, although much of its content had been written earlier for use in Europe. It was edited and republished in the later decades of the twentieth century by Henry Warner Bowden; see *Religion in America* (New York: Harper and Row Publishers, 1970).

11. Baird's broader interests were evident in publications such as *Impressions and Experiences of the West Indies and North America* (Philadelphia: Lea and Blanchard, 1850), *Sketches of Protestantism in Italy* (Boston: Perkins, 1845), and *Visit to Northern Europe* (New York: Taylor, 1841).

12. See Perry Miller, *The Life of the Mind in America from the Revolution to the Civil War* (New York: Harcourt, Brace and World, 1965), 40–48, where he compares insights into American society in the Jacksonian period.

13. Sydney Ahlstrom called attention to the importance of the Mercersburg Theology in his *Theology in America* (Indianapolis, Ind.: Bobbs-Merrill, 1967), chap. 8.

14. See James Hastings Nichols, *Romanticism in American Theology* (Chicago: University of Chicago Press, 1961) and *The Mercersburg Theology* (New York: Oxford University Press, 1966). His was an appreciative analysis of the project mounted by Nevin and Schaff. Nichols himself would have shied away from the term *cultural moment,* but it may be a useful designation to suggest how thoroughly focused it was in both its intensity and its boundedness.

15. George Shriver significantly contributed to the recovery of and

appreciation for Philip Schaff, especially through his *Philip Schaff: Christian Scholar and Ecumenical Prophet* (Macon, Ga.: Mercer University Press, 1987).

16. Another useful comprehensive introduction to Schaff was published by Klaus Penzel, ed., *Philip Schaff: Historical Ambassador of the Universal Church* (Macon, Ga.: Mercer University Press, 1991).

17. See Schaff, *America,* and Miller, *The Life of the Mind in America.*

18. Miller makes use of Schaff's essays to formulate the essential "voluntaryism" of American religion. Of course, the term has divergent connotations that make for recognition that it is a complex reality: the Latin root emphasizes the grounding in willpower or concerted action, and the English connotations imply its unconstrained quality.

19. Schaff's essay is "Church and State in the United States; or, The American Idea of Religious Liberty and Its Practical Effects," in *Papers of the American Historical Association,* vol. 2, no. 4 (New York: Putnam's, 1888).

20. Schaff was convinced that the forward movement of history would bring a reconciliation between Catholic and Protestant versions of Christianity. He termed this synthetic and much-to-be-desired outcome "evangelical Catholicism."

21. This project, published by the Christian Literature Company of New York, detailed the range of specific Christian denominations that had taken root in America, treating each as largely self-contained. Volume 1 was reissued by Scribner's in a revised and expanded version (taking account of the 1910 census) in 1912.

22. Bacon's concluding volume, along with Carroll's, indicates that, at least for a few scholars (presumably including Schaff as a general editor), more comprehensive categories were required to compass the topic adequately.

23. There has not been sufficient attention to the significance of the many seminaries and religious faculties, Catholic as well as Prot-

estant, that developed in the nineteenth century. Usually independent of the colleges and universities that were contemporary in their development, they were sites for significant although largely separate strands of learning, often having their own strong links to European traditions of thought. On the development of universities and the disciplines that took rise within them in post–Civil War America, see Jon H. Roberts and James Turner, *The Sacred and the Secular University* (Princeton, N.J.: Princeton University Press, 2000). At its beginning, the Divinity School stood at the center of the University of Chicago and as such had a very different sense of itself than other divinity schools linked to universities or free-standing (and typically denominational) seminaries. It is not accidental that self-conscious and critical historiography of religion in America had its initial flowering in the setting of Chicago. Conrad Cherry's recent study of the divinity schools delineates the Chicago program in a useful way; see his *Hurrying toward Zion: Universities, Divinity Schools and American Protestantism* (Bloomington: Indiana University Press, 1995).

24. Peter G. Mode, as will become evident, is a fascinating figure. My comments about him derive from informal conversations with several knowledgeable people but do not reflect detailed and necessarily precise information.

25. Peter G. Mode, *Sourcebook and Bibliographical Guide for American Church History* (Menasha, Wis.: George Banta, 1921).

26. Peter G. Mode, *The Frontier Spirit in American Christianity* (New York: Macmillan, 1923).

27. Henry K. Rowe, *The History of Religion in the United States* (New York: Macmillan, 1924).

28. William Warren Sweet's major textbook was titled *The Story of Religion in America* (New York: Harper and Row Publishers, 1950), deriving from an initial version entitled *The Story of Religions in America* (New York: Harper and Row Publishers,

1930). He also published several monographs on regions and/or periods as well as documentary compilations centering on the frontier's impact on denominations.

29. The chief collections of Sidney Mead's essays include *The Lively Experiment: The Shaping of Christianity in America* (New York: Harper and Row Publishers, 1963), *The Nation with the Soul of a Church* (New York: Harper and Row Publishers, 1975), and *The Old Religion in the Brave New World: Reflections on the Relation between Christendom and the Republic* (Berkeley: University of California Press, 1972).

30. In Mead's view, Roger Williams and Thomas Jefferson were the two points around which the ellipse of religious freedom was drawn that became the foundational principle for the United States.

31. For Schaff's vision, see especially "Church and State in the United States."

32. Clifton Olmstead, *History of Religion in the United States* (Englewood Cliffs, N.J.: Prentice-Hall, 1960). This book really stands for a new generation of literature that was published in the post–World War II period. All were "surveys" of religion in American history. In many respects, Olmstead's was less polished than several others, and it did not have their wide usage. But it does stand as a useful marker point, especially because it emphasizes the increased importance of college- or university-based scholars in the developing historiography about American religion.

33. Winthrop Hudson, *Religion in America: A Historical Account of the Development of American Religious Life* (New York: Charles Scribner's Sons, 1965). Hudson's durable volume went through successive revisions that had the effect of updating its materials and extending its reach as well as possibly recasting its implicit thesis. See the fifth edition, revised with John Corrigan (New York: Macmillan, 1992).

34. Conrad Cherry's book proved to be widely appreciated as a complement to the narrative accounts; see *God's New Israel: Religious Interpretations of American Destiny* (Englewood Cliffs, N.J.: Prentice-Hall, 1971).

35. H. Shelton Smith, Robert T. Handy, and Lefferts Loetscher, *American Christianity: An Historical Interpretation with Representative Documents,* vol. 1, 1607–1820 (New York: Charles Scribner's Sons, 1960); vol. 2, 1820–1960 (New York: Charles Scribner's Sons, 1963). This collaborative effort was exceptionally well crafted for a project involving several authors, and it reached out to incorporate a range of materials broader than the title might seem to imply; for example, volume 2 includes attention to the rise of religious humanism. While materials bearing on Catholic history are present, no attention is given to parallel Jewish developments. Its intended users were in the Protestant seminaries, while in fact much of the interest in the materials of American religion and scholarship about them was increasingly to be found in colleges and universities.

36. Martin E. Marty, *Righteous Empire: The Protestant Experience in America* (New York: Dial Press, 1970). This monograph, with its strong thesis, fits within the development of the broader literature that we have been chronicling.

37. Robert T. Handy, *A Christian America: Protestant Hopes and Historical Realities* (New York: Oxford University Press, 1971). Handy's volume is usefully compared to Marty's in terms of their respective and to some degree diverging definitions of periods and of problematics.

38. Will Herberg, *Protestant-Catholic-Jew: An Essay in American Religious Sociology* (Garden City, N.Y.: Anchor, 1960). Herberg's volume immediately captured attention. It was filled with anecdotes and incidents and replete with capsule summaries of the chief traditions he reviewed. In this sense, it was wonderfully suited for use in the classroom. Its more important point was to

reorient attention from denominations to the broad complex of religion in the culture (which included denominational religion, to be sure).

39. The following chapter makes reference to the article by Henry May that called attention to the important literature on religious topics and movements, largely written by general historians (in contrast to specialists in religious materials) that had been published in this same period. See "The Recovery of American Religious History," *American Historical Review* 70 (1964): 79–92.

40. Sydney Ahlstrom, *A Religious History of the American People* (New Haven, Conn.: Yale University Press, 1972). This volume was in preparation for many years, and generations of doctoral students, more than a few of whom contributed to its scope, finished their studies with Ahlstrom before it was completed.

41. At one level, this is a theoretical or conceptual issue. If the Puritan era was completed, was it succeeded by another distinctive epoch whose outline might be dimly perceived by a skilled interpreter? Or had that impulse in fact metamorphosed, for example, by having been taken up into—while at the same time itself contributing to the outcome of—a successor reality such as a secular era? At least to my mind, Sydney Ahlstrom did not fully address this issue, possibly because in the end it was not clear that the era he had denominated as "Protestant" had so decisively ended in the 1960s.

42. The place accorded to the Puritans in historiographical studies was reinforced by literary studies that found the literature of the Puritans a definitive starting point for American literature. Of course, Perry Miller himself was technically a professor of literature with an appointment to a department of English, not history (at Harvard).

43. This more inclusive and comprehensive framework—essentially that of the Atlantic world—has become commonplace in recent

decades. It can be traced back to such works as Winthrop Jordan's *White over Black: American Attitudes toward the Negro, 1550–1812* (Chapel Hill: University of North Carolina Press, 1968). This study raised troubling questions about the narrowness of the then-current starting point for so many studies of American cultural origins. In the decades since its publication, of course, the perspective has broadened greatly.

44. Large-scale immigration resumed after World War II following its dramatic decline, initially in response to World War I and then because of the restrictive policies that followed it. The renewal of immigration has reminded scholars that some of the resulting dynamics that were so pronounced in the nineteenth century were again manifest in the United States late in the twentieth century.

45. This foreshadows the later comments on the imaginative ideas of Marcus Lee Hansen that will be introduced and discussed briefly in chapter 3.

2. Religions in America

1. There is a strain of arbitrariness about such an effort, for interest in the subject has spread broadly through several disciplines, including specialists in religious historiography (of different stripes) as well as Americanists (both general historians and American studies types). Significant interest has also been demonstrated by sociologists and anthropologists. Among these different specialists (and others), there has been mutual interchange and learning, on the one hand, as well as significant resistance, on the other.

2. The *American Historical Review,* sponsored by the American Historical Association, is the leading journal of general historiography. Accordingly, the publication of the May essay in this periodical itself made an important point. See Henry May, "The

Recovery of American Religious History," *American Historical Review* 70 (1964): 79–92.

3. Numerous articles in early volumes of the *Review* manifested a bias toward the history of institutions. Accordingly, many of them were devoted to political and religious subjects, since governments and religious institutions are among the most reliable repositories of official and trustworthy records.

4. The American Society of Church History is a "sibling" professional society to the American Historical Association. Originally formed at the same time, it incorporated some of the same figures as active members. Its history has been chronicled by Henry Warner Bowden in several studies that chart its fortunes across a century and more. See the references in note 9, chapter 1.

The American Catholic Historical Association has a different principle of organization. It is largely a professional society for those practicing historians who are Catholic and who may or may not be studying that tradition. Membership in the American Society of Church History rests on the nature of the subject matter, while membership in the American Catholic Historical Association primarily rests on the common religious association of its members.

5. One reason for the attention to Puritan and Protestant topics in the literature about religion in American history is the searching and powerful analysis of early American literature and culture that derived from the interests and work of Perry Miller, boosted by the influence deriving from Max Weber's work, especially the essays translated by Talcott Parsons and published as *The Protestant Ethic and the Spirit of Capitalism* (London: Allen and Unwin, 1930). In the last decades of the twentieth century, a number of excellent studies of other traditions, especially Catholicism, restored some greater balance to the literature. An early prominent example of these later studies is Robert Orsi, *The Madonna of 115th Street* (New Haven, Conn.: Yale University

Press, 1985). It is noteworthy that Emil Durkheim's rather different inspiration for work in the social sciences had intervened by that time.

6. Catherine Albanese, *Sons of the Fathers: The Civil Religion of the American Revolution* (Philadelphia: Temple University Press, 1976).

7. Catherine Albanese, *Corresponding Motion: Transcendental Religion and the New America* (Philadelphia: Temple University Press, 1977).

8. Catherine Albanese, *America: Religions and Religion* (Belmont, Calif.: Wadsworth, 1981). This book was explicitly designed as a textbook, was clearly intended for use in courses, and is demonstrably useful as class reading. In this it contrasted with Ahlstrom's megavolume, which obviously had grown from the author's teaching at Yale but had outgrown any simple identity as a textbook.

9. Albanese's volume clearly reflects a post-Protestant understanding of America and especially the religious life of Americans.

10. In their scholarship, both Ahlstrom and Albanese were, quite literally, fascinated by the range of religious expression in the United States. For the former, the extent and diversity of religious phenomena were best interpreted within a broad (rather than narrow) overall theme—the great four hundred–year Protestant Era that he believed might have already ended. For the latter, the same given (the extent and diversity of religious phenomena) drove her to take a broader interest in the diversity of religion in the culture.

11. To frame her work, Albanese drew on the theoretical reflection that had been shaped by the history of religions scholars at the University of Chicago.

12. At least as taken over into the writing of American religious history, the influence that derived from the social sciences might be viewed as preferred templates that privileged certain narrative

structures. This conferred importance on certain kinds of data as well as highlighting particular questions or approaches to research concerning that data. But it was the narrative structures, more than the templates taken as directing a research agenda, that proved the more important for historiography. In these terms, substituting several narratives for a single overarching or controlling one did not affect the idiom; rather, it was a strategy for dealing with differences and acknowledging pluralism. So the significance of narrative in the development of new impulses in religious historiography was simply that this mode of presenting a case remained fundamental, as it has in historiography considered more generally.

13. Thomas Tweed, ed., *Retelling U.S. Religious History* (Berkeley: University of California Press, 1997). Tweed has proved to be a catalyst in the story told here, possibly in part because he entered the field with a special, partly nomadic, perspective. While his formal graduate work was done at Stanford in the Department of Religious Studies, he lost his mentor, William Clebsch, before his degree was completed. Clebsch hewed to an unconventional path in the field, undoubtedly encouraging his students' iconoclasm. Tweed reached out to others, like William R. Hutchison at Harvard, for assistance in completing his degree, but he also undertook to be instructed by and to learn from a range of specialists, so this book, and the project from which it derived, was a manifestation of his own career development.

This may be an appropriate point at which to note the role played by the Lilly Endowment over several decades in providing grants to support a number of historical projects. Following Lilly's lead, the Pew Charitable Trusts has also supported significant historical work, the project led by Thomas Tweed being one among many. It is also important to stress that this group of scholars exemplifies the collaboration that characterizes a new style of historiography in this as in some other special fields.

14. These motifs are summarized on pages 17–19 in ibid.

15. The "sites" explicitly include sexuality, ritual, women's roles, and "supply-side" considerations.

16. Tweed, ed., *Retelling U.S. Religious History*, 1–23. In general, this discussion exhibits great sensitivity.

17. Ibid., 17 ff.

18. Roger Finke's contribution derived from his collaboration with Rodney Stark, a sociologist of distinction, with whom he published a jointly authored book, *The Churching of America, 1776–1990* (New Brunswick, N.J.: Rutgers University Press, 1990). Stark's own interests in religion have ranged very widely indeed, beginning with the influence of his own teacher, Charles Y. Glock, and including serious interest in religion in late antiquity.

19. Albanese's essay presents themes that are very close to those that provided structure to her textbook, *America: Religions and Religion,* discussed above.

20. Harry S. Stout and Daryl G. Hart, eds., *New Directions in American Religious History* (New York: Oxford University Press, 1997).

21. The project from which this volume derived was a one-time conference without the provision for repeated continuing interaction among the authors, a condition that made the Tweed-led undertaking so highly collaborative.

22. The book has four major parts, each of which includes "Protestant" or some variation thereof in the title, indicating, if not a restriction of subject matter, then a basic reference point for the whole. To be sure, the last part is entitled "Protestants and Outsiders" and includes essays about African Americans, Roman Catholics, and Jews. If nothing else, however, the preponderance of attention to Protestantism as the axis of the field indicates that Ahlstrom's premonition that the Protestant Era was ending in the 1960s was not necessarily accepted by historians working in

the field who succeeded him, and it certainly did not constrain them.

23. It may be useful to suggest that Henry May's perspective on the "recovery" of interest in American religion informs the Stout and Hart volume even as history of religions perspectives underlie the Tweed volume.

24. This set of concluding essays might be termed the "caboose effect," through which the cars conveying the payload of the train are trailed by a terminal work car equipped to deal with the unexpected. To change to a more felicitous image, the major template of the Protestant-derived chapters is qualified by an acknowledgment that in the end one size does not fit all.

25. The preceding comments in the text and notes should not be read as disparaging the range and reach of the essays that comprise the volume, for they direct attention to economic, political, and cultural themes that succeed in significantly broadening the subject of religion in American history. In this sense, as suggested above, a shadow from the story Henry May recounted falls over the project and the book.

26. In effect, the point is that narrative accounts, or constructed stories, remain such even when rendered as plural and codependent. The basic modality in which the historiography of American religion is presented has not changed, even though it may well have been rendered with more dimensions and in greater complexity.

27. To some extent, it might be argued that the history of religions inspiration that underlay the Tweed project included such an approach. This discussion, however, points to the more fundamental contribution to enrichment of historical studies that came directly from social sciences, especially anthropology and sociology, rather than indirectly by means of the history of religions school.

28. Peter Williams is singled out because, with a shifting set of colleagues, he drew inspiration more directly from social sciences literature than from history of religions perspectives.

29. Peter Williams, *Popular Religion in America* (Englewood Cliffs, N.J.: Prentice-Hall, 1980) was conceived as a critically appreciative response to the Ahlstrom opus.

30. This strand of social theorizing has been particularly significant in the development of twentieth-century anthropological interest in religion, perhaps because it focused on collectivities and the cultures they produced. Thus attention necessarily turned to the role of religion in understanding the behavior of groups.

31. Weber's legacy with respect to the historical understanding of religion has had more direct influence in terms of diachronic casting of questions, of which the foremost has been that of secularization.

32. Representative publications by these figures are listed in subsequent notes.

33. Parsons's role in conveying the import of this tradition of European social thought cannot be overestimated, since it operated through his publications and, more important, because he trained (directly and indirectly) generations of graduate students who went on to become extremely influential. He had translated into English and published Max Weber's *The Protestant Ethic and the Spirit of Capitalism*.

34. An exception to this statement might be Anthony F. C. Wallace. He provided specific studies of religion (e.g., introducing the concept of "revitalization movement" that has been so widely appropriated; see "Revitalization Movements," *American Anthropologist* 58 [1956]: 264–81), but he also published an influential textbook, *Religion: An Anthropological View* (New York: Random House, 1966). So Wallace at once theorized at the microlevel about the research he was doing (such as concerning a particular revitalization movement) but also provided a compre-

hensive overview. While the latter is presented abstractly, it does reinforce the observation that those who propose to understand this dimension or segment of human life, individual and collective, must attend to the full range of religious phenomena.

35. See Wallace, "Revitalization Movements."

36. Revitalization impulses are often expressed through and codified in millenarian movements. See studies such as Kenelm Burridge, *New Heavens, New Earth* (Oxford: Blackwell, 1969) and Michael Adas, *Prophets of Rebellion* (Chapel Hill: University of North Carolina Press, 1979).

37. William McLoughlin, *Revivals, Awakenings, and Reform: An Essay on Religion and Social Change in America, 1607–1977* (Chicago: University of Chicago Press, 1978).

38. Robert William Fogel, *The Fourth Great Awakening and the Future of Egalitarianism* (Chicago: University of Chicago Press, 2000).

39. The point, of course, is that a historian's use of such a model differs from how it frames the work of a social scientist. For the latter, the significance lies in the comparability of phenomena (which may even be conceived as comprising a genre or class), while for the former the insight that broadly comparable phenomena exist tutors the historian in his or her research into unique subjects.

40. The essay, "Center and Periphery," is easily consulted in Edward Shils, *The Constitution of Society* (Chicago: University of Chicago Press, 1982), 93–109.

41. The term "denominational society" provided the title for Andrew Greeley's study of American society in its religious aspects; see *The Denominational Society* (Glenview, Ill.: Scott, Foresman, 1972). In this sense, it followed in the lineage of studies such as Will Herberg, *Protestant-Catholic-Jew: An Essay in American Religious Sociology* (Garden City, N.Y.: Anchor, 1960) and Gerhard Lenski, *The Religious Factor* (Garden City, N.Y.: Double-

day, 1961), earlier attempts to frame American society in religious terms.

42. This was a strong theme in the writings of Peter Berger. His most widely used work in the sociology of religion was probably *The Sacred Canopy* (Garden City, N.Y.: Doubleday, 1969), although *The Social Construction of Reality* (Garden City, N.Y.: Doubleday, 1966) had great influence among practicing historians.

43. Of course, Roger Finke participated in the Tweed project. *The Churching of America*, written with Rodney Stark, carries this line of reasoning (among others) to a strong conclusion that typically has been resisted by historians.

44. In other words, not all social science concepts stand on equal footing, some being much more precise and limited, others being broader in scope. The full range of social scientific thought has indeed exercised very significant influence over historians, albeit in individual and different ways.

45. This is the other side of the point made in the preceding note, namely that terms and concepts have a precise significance in sociological theory. When highly theorized terms (e.g., *secularization*) are used by historians, they inevitably exert subliminal pressure back upon those who employ them to require greater exactitude and more careful selection of terms. So even historians who may fail to appreciate the scholarship of social scientists find themselves in thrall to them as their discourse and work are shared with others in the narrow guild, let alone as they reach more broadly to a general public.

46. The specific reference is to Clifford Geertz, whose work has had such a great impact on historiographical study as to lie virtually beyond measurement. The term is one he coined, as in "thick description."

47. If anything, commitment to the plurality of stories and making use of the work of social scientists has only reconfirmed histori-

ans in their use of narrative, an outcome not unrelated, perhaps, to the fascination with "story" in culture more generally. Indeed, social scientists have also resorted to narration in their most influential work; for example, Clifford Geertz is a master storyteller.

48. This may signal the next opportunity in expanding the scope of historical study of religion in the United States. One example might be Jay Demerath's recently published *Crossing the Gods: World Religions and Worldly Politics* (New Brunswick, N.J.: Rutgers University Press, 2001).

49. A partial exception to this generalization was in the attempt to explore Mexican civil religion as a reference point for the understanding of that topic in the U.S. case. See, for example, Philip E. Hammond, "The Conditions for Civil Religion: A Comparison of the United States and Mexico," in Philip Hammond and Robert Bellah, eds., *Varieties of Civil Religion* (San Francisco, Calif.: Harper and Row Publishers, 1980). Robert T. Handy compiled a "comparative account" of religion in North America (Canada and the United States) that exemplifies an older and typical historians' approach. See *A History of the Churches in the United States and Canada* (New York: Oxford University Press, 1977).

3. Religion(s) of America

1. Marcus Lee Hansen, *The Atlantic Migration, 1607–1860* (Cambridge, Mass.: Harvard University Press, 1940).

2. The influential historian Oscar Handlin took up the challenge of studying immigration to America as the beginning point for historical study of this society. He linked it to liberty as the great theme of American history.

3. With respect to the religious dimension of migration, Timothy L. Smith offered the insight that it was critical to understand the

religions of migrating communities in the cultures of origin as well as after arrival in the New World.

4. See Marcus Lee Hansen, "Immigration and Puritanism," *Norwegian-American Studies and Records* 9 (1936): 1–28.

5. By turning the question around, so to speak, and suggesting that the Puritan experience might be seen as paradigmatic for successor immigrant communities, Hansen offered an insight that in principle opened the subject of Puritanism to be studied in a new comparative fashion.

6. The "three generation hypothesis" proposed by Hansen has enjoyed a long career in classrooms as well as in social studies.

7. Will Herberg, *Protestant-Catholic-Jew: An Essay in American Religious Sociology* (Garden City, N.Y.: Anchor, 1960). Herberg not only contributed to understanding the role and place of religion in American society but also came to embrace his own Jewish traditions in ways that led to an interesting attempt to formulate them for the use of the Jewish community in America. See *Judaism and Modern Man: An Interpretation of Jewish Religion* (New York: Farrar, Straus, and Giroux, 1951).

8. Many of Herberg's interests were carried on by sociologists of religion. For example, Gerhard Lenski's *The Religious Factor* (Garden City, N.Y.: Doubleday, 1961) was based on extensive data and much fuller and systematic analysis of them. Robert Bellah's interests led to the collaborative *Habits of the Heart: Individualism and Commitment in American Life* (Berkeley: University of California Press, 1985). A succeeding generation of scholars has been prolific in exploring religion in American society; see, for instance, among the many studies by Robert Wuthnow, *The Restructuring of American Religion* (Princeton, N.J.: Princeton University Press, 1988) and by N. J. Demerath, *A Bridging of Faiths: Religion and Politics in a New England City* (Princeton, N.J.: Princeton University Press, 1992).

9. *The Lonely Crowd* was written with Nathan Glazer and Reuel

Denney and originally published by Yale University Press in 1950. An abridged edition was issued in 1956 (Garden City, N.Y.: Doubleday). This study was immensely influential in the 1950s.

10. This expansive application of "Hansen's Law" was central to Herberg's interpretive essay.

11. One fundamental theme insufficiently noted in the interpretation of American religion is that, at least in the context of American society, the expression of social identities in religious (as opposed to other) terms is nonthreatening. It is, if you will, a coded means of announcing that the uniqueness that means a great deal to me (or to us) does not threaten you. An interesting exhibit of this phenomenon concerns the Black Muslims, a religiously cast identity for a group whose early social program might more accurately have been politically labeled "Black Nationalism." Such an identity would have seemed to challenge the majority society and thus raise fundamental questions about the group's loyalty to the American nation. Thus the religious frame of reference deflected such concerns.

12. This assertion is based upon innumerable Gallup surveys that consistently report much higher rates of religious observance or practice on the part of, as well as in the significance of beliefs to, America's population than is the case, for example, within European societies. One issue is whether in asking the same questions across different societies there are comparable connotations as well as denotations. If the significance does broadly correlate, that only transposes the question to become why religion is valued more or less, or understood variously, in different societies that otherwise share many elements of culture.

13. This being the case helps to explain why importance is attached to historical study of it.

14. It is important to emphasize that Herberg's was not a reductive use of models or social scientific paradigms. Accordingly, he was not attempting to formulate a "total explanation," and in prin-

ciple his approach would allow for supplementation as well as differential weighting of factors. Of course, his was also a "loose application" of social science, and he was not conducting research or analyzing extensive data sets. In short, his interpretive, even journalistic or impressionistic, use of social science thus readily opened toward historiographical endeavors.

15. As the interest in civil religion intensified, stimulated by Robert Bellah's proposal, Herberg clearly thought that there was a failure to give him adequate credit for having already explored this phenomenon under a slightly different title. See his essay, "America's Civil Religion: What It Is and Whence It Comes," in Russell E. Richey and Donald G. Jones, *American Civil Religion* (New York: Harper and Row Publishers, 1974), 76–88.

16. Ancient Rome is the frequent reference point, possibly because Jewish life and practice were tolerated within the empire even as Christians came to be persecuted. Of course, Christianity itself became the religion of the empire under Constantine. An interesting question concerns the possibility that there are other kinds of religious grounding of social orders, and if so, if they should not also be kept in view. See Jay Demerath, *Crossing the Gods: World Religions and Worldly Politics* (New Brunswick, N.J.: Rutgers University Press, 2001) for an attempt to find comparable or analogous functions for religion among very different social orders where it is readily assumed that differences are salient.

17. Durkheim's great work was *The Elementary Forms of the Religious Life* (London: Unwin, 1915; New York: Free Press, 1965). In recent decades, his ideas may have had their greater impact on historians of religious subjects in America through the work of a figure like Mary Douglas, whose *Natural Symbols* (New York: Pantheon Books, 1970) had immense influence, especially in the 1970s and 1980s.

18. This subtheme of *Protestant-Catholic-Jew* marks the volume as

a radical critique of American culture. This side of the book received little attention in scholarly circles. Of course, it was a posture directly at odds with the theme of American civil religion, which evaluated the American Way of Life in much more positive terms.

19. Herberg's "equivocality" may be the book's most significant trait.

20. Robert Bellah's essay, "Civil Religion in America," was initially published in *Daedalus,* the journal of the American Academy of Arts and Sciences, in its special issue *Religion in America* (winter 1967): 1–21. The essay was also delivered as a lecture at an annual meeting of the American Academy of Religion.

21. The essay suggested a broader program but did not itself demonstrate what the results of such a full-fledged study would look like. For an example of a skeptical review of the project, see John F. Wilson, "The Status of 'Civil Religion' in America," in *The Religion of the Republic,* ed. Elwyn Smith (Philadelphia: Fortress, 1971). Of course, others have tried to apply it in various ways, although none demonstrated its secure existence.

22. The literature on civil religion was vast. Among some of the many relevant publications are Robert Bellah, *The Broken Covenant* (New York: Seabury Press, 1975; 2nd ed., Chicago: University of Chicago Press, 1992); John M. Cuddihy, *No Offense: Civil Religion and Protestant Taste* (New York: Seabury Press, 1978); Catherine Albanese, *Sons of the Fathers* (Philadelphia: Temple University Press, 1976); and John F. Wilson, *Public Religion in American Culture* (Philadelphia: Temple University Press, 1979).

23. One interesting line of inquiry has been followed most consistently, and insistently, by Edward Linenthal, whose studies of public commemoration are extremely useful. See his *Sacred Ground* (Urbana: University of Illinois Press, 1991). See also Edward Linenthal and David Chidester, eds., *American Sacred Space* (Bloomington: Indiana University Press, 1995).

24. This judgment was expressed in the initial paragraph of the original essay; see Bellah, "Civil Religion in America."

25. Obvious examples would be the assassination of a president or other major figure (such as John F. and possibly Robert Kennedy or conceivably Martin Luther King Jr.) or a sharply focused political crisis (for example, the widespread belief among a younger generation that the United States was mired in Southeast Asia in the 1960s and early 1970s or the terrorist attacks launched on the United States on September 11, 2001).

26. This is the specific lineage attributed to it by Harold Bloom in the book to be discussed in the next paragraphs.

27. Harold Bloom, *The American Religion* (New York: Simon and Schuster, 1992).

28. Ibid., 32.

29. Gnosticism is a highly complex subject. Since Bloom accepts this label, it seems appropriate to use it about him and his work. But that move may beg the precise meaning of the term, and in the course of a long history it has been used to identify many different specific figures and movements that might be thought to have little in common.

30. From one point of view, Bloom undertakes to rest his case on the seemingly most resistant of instances by selecting these two exhibits. In effect, he identifies American religion with assertive individualism and by means of that correlation turns these "hard cases" into a powerful argument for the pervasiveness of *the* American religion. The counterquestion may then become whether individualism in American society necessarily carries a religious dimension or spiritual reference, especially in a consumption-driven society. I would argue that only if individualism entails a collective dimension along with its ecstatic emphasis should it be interpreted as "religious."

31. See the recent study of Cane Ridge by Paul Conkin, *Cane Ridge:*

America's Pentecost (Madison: University of Wisconsin Press, 1990). It may be important to resist this easy judgment that Cane Ridge is such a clear-cut beginning point. See the very important study by Leigh Eric Schmidt, *Holy Fairs: Scottish Communions and American Revivals in the Early Modern Period* (Princeton, N.J.: Princeton University Press, 1989). In his perspective, Cane Ridge should be seen more as a culmination of earlier trends than as a decisive new beginning, as in birthing an American religion à la Bloom.

32. See note 30, which begins to introduce this question.

33. Ecstasy is taken to be a generic aspect of human experience, and in a more specifically religious perspective it links to assertions that there is a transcendent reference for life that is relevant to human existence. Recent discussion of this phenomenon started with I. M. Lewis, *Ecstatic Religion: An Anthropological Study* (Harmondsworth, England: Penguin Books, 1971).

34. This dialectical relationship I take to be definitive with respect to whether religion is present or absent. Without both elements being present and interacting, I take it to be difficult to argue convincingly that religion is present.

35. W. Lloyd Warner, *Yankee City Series,* 5 vols. (New Haven, Conn.: Yale University Press, 1941–59). Warner's work represents another conduit through which Durkheim's ideas were introduced to the American intellectual world. *The Living and the Dead* (volume 5, 1959) is the most directly relevant to our consideration of American religion. A one-volume version was issued as *The Family of God* (New Haven, Conn.: Yale University Press, 1961). It incorporated the chapters and sections of the Yankee City study most relevant to Yankee City's manifest symbolic life that might be construed as religious.

36. Lloyd Warner, *American Life: Dream and Reality* (Chicago: University of Chicago Press, 1953; reprint, 1962) presents several

independent essays that explore different aspects of social behavior in the United States at mid–twentieth century. For Warner's comments on mass media, see pages 247–73.

37. This horizontal integration of the media has been widely remarked upon in recent years. "Horizontal integration" I take to mean the interpenetration of news and views, entertainment and fashion, philanthropy and commercialism. There is a logic to this intentionally explicit melding of different aspects of culture since, viewed analytically, the integration is in fact reality. What Americans may be predisposed to think of as differentiated elements are in reality aspects of one culture.

38. David M. Potter, *People of Plenty* (Chicago: University of Chicago Press, 1954). Potter's work was in many respects ahead of its time. Contemporary social analysis might benefit from recovering and applying some of his insights.

39. Benedict Anderson gave special utility to this term in his study, *Imagined Communities: Reflections on the Origin and Spread of Nationalism* (London: Verso, 1983; 2nd ed., London: Verso, 1991).

INDEX

Index

Index

Index